World's Best Magic Tricks

Charles Barry Townsend

Sterling Publishing Co., Inc.   New York

Dedication

To three of my oldest friends, and golf partners:
Vinny Enright, Jack Chambers, and Ernie
Flemming. I miss those matches we played on
the rolling hills of New Jersey and all the hours
that were spent on the 19th hole.

Library of Congress Cataloging-in-Publication Data

Townsend, Charles Barry.
    World's best magic tricks / Charles Barry Townsend.
        p.   cm.
    Includes index.
    ISBN 0-8069-8582-8
    1. Conjuring.   2. Tricks.   I. Title.
  GV1547.T65   1992
  793.8—dc20   91-41310
                                             CIP

10 9 8 7 6 5 4

First paperback edition published in 1993 by
Sterling Publishing Company, Inc.
387 Park Avenue South, New York, N.Y. 10016
© 1992 by Charles Barry Townsend
Distributed in Canada by Sterling Publishing
% Canadian Manda Group, P.O. Box 920, Station U
Toronto, Ontario, Canada M8Z 5P9
Distributed in Great Britain and Europe by Cassell PLC
Villiers House, 41/47 Strand, London WC2N 5JE, England
Distributed in Australia by Capricorn Link Ltd.
P.O. Box 665, Lane Cove, NSW 2066
Manufactured in the United States of America
All rights reserved

Sterling ISBN 0-8069-8582-8 Trade
              0-8069-8583-6 Paper

CONTENTS

• •

INTRODUCTION

To my way of thinking, performing magic tricks is the greatest hobby in the world. Very few pastimes have such a rich and diverse body of literature. Well over 100,000 books have been published on the subject in the past 150 years.

People love to be fooled—to pretend, if only for a little while, that the impossible is possible. And almost anything can be used in a magical way to confound and outwit an audience. If you look through magic dealers' catalogues, you will find tricks that revolve around cards, liquids, balls, coins, flowers, stage illusions, ropes, escapes, mental magic, close-up or table magic, thimbles, steel rings, spook shows, dice, silks, hypnotism, comedy magic, and balloons. Within these diverse categories, hundreds of different everyday items will be magically manipulated to float, to appear, to disappear, or to change position, color, or size.

The mechanics of performing an illusion are, of course, important. Every movement must be smooth and sure. The magician must practice each trick over and over again until he can execute it flawlessly, without consciously thinking about it. Once he achieves this, he can then turn to the real challenge of being entertaining.

The story associated with the presentation of any trick should be interesting, plausible, and whenever possible, witty. In any magic program it is always desirable to have audience participation. Comedy is another ingredient that adds greatly to any performance. However, do not create comedy at the expense of making a volunteer feel ridiculous.

As has been stated so often before, the best magician is an actor playing the part of a magician. The next time David Copperfield, Mark Wilson, Harry Blackstone, Ricky Jay, Carl Ballantine, or Doug Henning performs on television, watch him closely and observe how he presents each trick. As the old song says, "It ain't what you do, it's the way that you do it!"

The 48 tricks presented in this book are truly outstanding examples of the art of legerdemain. The execution of each one is well within the capabilities of the average reader. Secret methods are subtly used to execute the tricks.

You will find enough material in this book to put two or three shows together. There are also tricks that can be used in impromptu situations. Only two tricks call for the construction of special boxes; all of the other tricks use common materials found around the home, such as rope, cards, and water glasses.

In closing, I wish you every success in staging the many fine feats contained herein. You should get as much pleasure from performing them as your audience will get out of watching them. As I said before, magic is a wonderful hobby, one that once taken up is impossible to ever be free of again. Who would want to be?

Charles Barry Townsend

Silk Magic

THE FAMOUS SYMPATHETIC SILK SCARVES MYSTERY

Effect

On the table is a thin wooden stand, four silk scarves, and two water glasses. Stand behind the table and say: "On this table I have four large silk scarves, two red and two white, draped over the arms of this wooden stand (Fig. 1). First, I take the two red scarves from the stand and tie them together, using one corner of each scarf. These two scarves are now placed in the glass with the card leaning against it which reads *knotted*. I now remove the two white scarves and place them in the glass with the card which reads *unknotted*.

"Now for a little bit of magic. I transpose the cards, placing the *knotted* card in front of the glass with the white scarves, and the *unknotted* card in front of the glass with the red scarves. Would you believe that the knot has also moved from one glass to the other? Well, it has! See, I remove the red scarves from the glass and they are no longer tied together, while over here, the white scarves are so tightly tied that it will take some effort to get them apart. Wonderful, isn't it?"

Materials Needed

Four 18-inch-square silk scarves, two red and two white
Two water glasses
Two printed cards
Wooden stand to hang the silk scarves on

Preparation

The wooden stand is easy to build and stands about 16 inches high. Paint the center rod black with white ends like a wand.

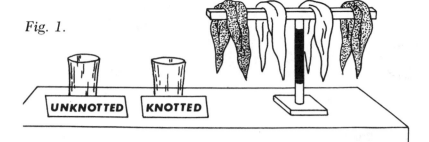

Fig. 1.

UNKNOTTED   KNOTTED

Paint the base black and white. The crossbar measures
¾″ × ¾″ × 16″ long. Paint it jet black. It should have a deep
channel running along the top. Cover the ends of the crossbar
so that the channel is not apparent to the onlooker (Fig. 2).

The secret of the white knot literally rests in the channel of
the crossbar. In setting the stand up for presentation, take the
two white silk scarves and knot them tightly together. Then,
using a pencil, push the knot down into the channel at the
midway point. Push two inches more of each scarf down into
the channel on either side of the knot. Now, drape half of each
scarf over the front and back of the bar (Fig. 3). Finally, drape
the two red scarves over the ends of the bar.

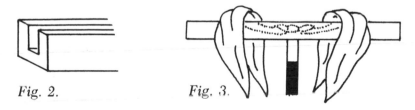

Fig. 2.

Fig. 3.

Presentation

There are two major steps involved in presenting this trick.
First, when you tie the two red scarves together, use a false
knot to secure them. The knot looks genuine, but it can be
easily pulled apart (Figs. 4 and 5). After tying the knot, roll
the scarves into a ball and place them in the glass labelled
knotted. While rolling them up, secretly pull the knot apart.

Step two deals with removing the white scarves from the

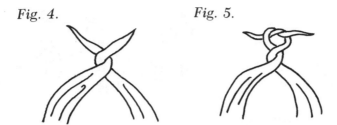

Fig. 4.　　　　　Fig. 5.

stand. Pick up the trailing ends of both scarves, one with each hand, and raise them above the bar (Fig. 6). Now, transfer the end in your right hand to your left hand. Next, put your right hand around both scarves and slide it down towards the bar. Just as it reaches the bar, pull both scarves upwards, with your left hand, just enough so that the knotted section comes out of the channel in the bar (Fig. 7). This action is too quick to be seen, and is covered by the back of your right hand.

Now, drop the ends of the scarves and roll them into a ball and tuck them into the glass marked *unknotted*. The mechanics of the trick are now finished. The final magical presentation is up to you.

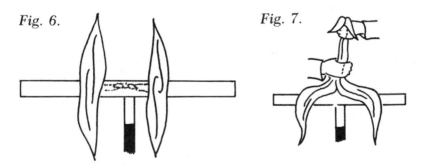

Fig. 6.　　　　　Fig. 7.

THE PENETRATING SILK SCARF

Effect
Pick up a brightly colored silk scarf at its two opposite corners and thread it through the space beneath the top bar of a

folding chair. Then bring the ends of the silk scarf together and pull them both upwards and apart. The center of the silk scarf seemingly melts through the wooden bar.

Then repeat the effect a second time. Ask a spectator to hold up a solid Hula Hoop while you wrap the silk scarf around its opposite side. Once again the silk scarf, when pulled towards you, seems to melt through the solid ring.

Materials Needed

One 18-inch-square colored silk scarf
A length of strong black thread
A wooden folding chair
A solid Hula Hoop
A table

Preparation

Lay out the silk scarf on the table. Tie one end of the thread to a corner of the silk scarf, and the other end to the corner diagonally opposite to it.

Presentation

Thread the silk scarf through the space below the top bar of the chair, as shown in Fig. 8. Note that the thumb of the left hand is on top of the thread at corner B, while the thumb and fingers of the right hand are under the thread at corner A.

Now, bring your two hands together above the top of the chair, as shown in Fig. 9. At this point, hook the thumb of

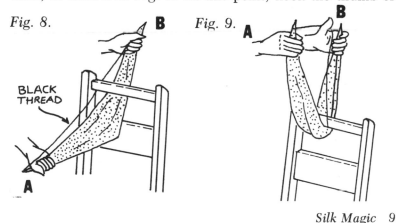

Fig. 8.   B   Fig. 9.   A   B

BLACK THREAD

A

your left hand under the thread at point *A*. The remaining
fingers of your left hand should be holding the corner of the
silk.

Now comes the critical movement. Release corner *B* of the
silk scarf and move your hands rapidly apart. The thread will
quickly wrap the corner of the silk scarf around the chair bar
and bring it back into your left hand (Fig. 10).

The action is so quick that it appears that the silk scarf
melted right through the bar. Practice these movements many
times until they work smoothly and there is no hesitation on
your part. When mastered, this is a completely convincing
illusion.

Fig. 10.

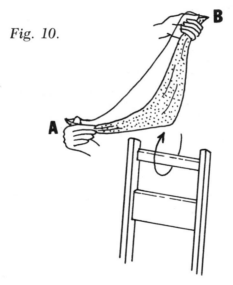

To vary the presentation, first pass the silk through the bar
of the chair two or three times. Then request a spectator to
assist you for a final test of the Penetrating Silk. Have him first
examine a large Hula Hoop, and then instruct him to hold it
up perpendicular to the floor about waist high. Then thread
the silk through the hoop (Fig. 11) and bring the ends together, as you did before, to secure the thread with your right
thumb (Fig. 12).

Fig. 11.

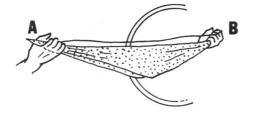

Fig. 12.

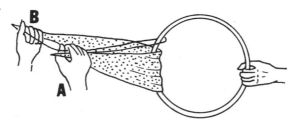

Now, instruct him, on the count of three, to pull the hoop towards himself. At that moment, release the end of the silk held in your right hand and spread your hands apart; this will cause the end of the silk scarf to fly around the inside of the hoop and come back to your right hand. This is the same action that you used in making the silk scarf penetrate the chair bar.

At this point, thank the spectator for his help and acknowledge the applause from the audience.

Table Magic

THE THINK-A-DRINK TRICK

Effect

Place six white business-sized cards on the table. Printed on the face of each card is the name of a popular drink (Fig. 13). Instruct a member of the audience to mentally select one of the drinks. After he has done so, ask him to silently spell the name of the drink to himself, one letter at a time, as you tap each card in turn. Every time you tap a card, your assistant is to spell one letter. When your assistant reaches the last letter of the drink, he is to cry, "Stop!" To his astonishment, you will be pointing at the card with the name of his drink on it.

Materials Needed

Six white business cards. On each card should be printed, in large letters, the name of a popular drink: *tea*, *milk*, *water*, *coffee*, *limeade*, and *root beer*.

Fig. 13.

Presentation

The secret of the trick lies in the fact that the names of the drinks all contain a different number of letters. Tea has three, milk has four, water has five, etc. After your assistant has mentally chosen one of the drinks, instruct him to spell out the name of his drink, one letter at a time, as you touch each card in turn. For the first two letters, you can touch any of the cards. However, starting with the third letter, you must touch the three-letter card, *tea*, for the fourth letter the card *milk*, for the fifth letter the word *water*, etc., until the spectator says "Stop!"

When you place the cards on the table, mix them up so that the fact that each drink contains a different number of letters is not obvious. Also, use this trick more as a transition from one major trick to another. Do it once and don't repeat it, as the modus operandi will quickly become apparent if repeated too often.

You can also make up a set of these cards using objects other than drinks. You might use colors, rock stars, cars, etc. Tailor the cards to suit your audience.

THE CLEVER CLOCK TRICK
. . . .

Effect

Show a piece of paper, with the face of a clock on it, to a member of the audience and ask him to mentally select one of the numbers on it. Tell him to add one to the number and to start counting at that number when you start tapping your pencil on the clock dial.

He is to continue counting silently to himself every time you tap the pencil on the paper until he reaches 20. At this point, he is to say "Stop." You then circle a number on the clock dial and hand him the paper face down, instructing him to tell the audience what number he originally chose. When he turns the paper over, he will see that you have correctly circled the number he had picked out.

Materials Needed
A drawing of a face of a clock on a sheet of paper, and xerox copies of this drawing to be used when you perform this trick in the future

Presentation
The trick is simple to do, and can be repeated any number of times. When you start tapping your pencil on the paper, start at number seven and go counterclockwise around the dial. Don't let anyone see where you start. When the participant reaches 20, and calls "Stop," your pencil will be on the chosen number. Circle it and turn the sheet upside down before handing it to him. It works every time!

THE GLASS-THROUGH-THE-TABLE BAFFLEMENT
• •

Effect
While sitting behind a table, place a coin on the table and remark: "I am now going to show you an experiment in Mind-Over-Matter! Note that this coin is heads up on the table." Then place an inverted water glass over it and cover the glass with a sheet of newspaper, creating in effect a paper cone.

"I want everyone to concentrate on the coin and visualize it turning over on the table. Very good! Your minds are very strong. I think that the coin is now tails up." Lift the paper and glass together, and everyone looks at the coin, which is still heads up.

"I guess I was wrong," you continue. "Let's try it again." Then place the covered glass back over the coin. After a moment or two, exclaim, "This is never going to work! You're thinking about the glass, not the coin!" With that, smash your hand down on top of the paper, which crumbles to the table. The glass has disappeared. Reach under the table and bring out the glass, saying, "You caused the glass to go right through the table!"

Materials Needed

One heavy water glass
A square of newspaper or a stiff napkin
One silver quarter

Presentation

The trick is as described in the above **Effect** section up to the point where you lift the paper cone and glass together to check the coin underneath. As you bend over to look at the coin, move the paper and glass back past the edge of the table and let the glass slide out and drop into your lap (Fig. 14). The top of the table will effectively hide this action. Without pausing more than a second, move your hand, with the paper shell, back towards the coin. The stiff paper will retain its shape and look as though the glass is still under it.

Place the paper over the coin and drop your right hand into your lap. Smash your left hand down on the paper cone, making everyone at the table jump in surprise. While they are

Fig. 14.

wondering where the glass went, take the glass from your lap with your right hand and pretend that you caught it going through the bottom of the table.

This is an old but very effective trick that catches everyone by surprise due to the misdirection concerning the idea of turning a coin over with mind power.

THE BALANCING-GLASS MYSTERY

Effect

During an interlude at the dinner table, take a half-full glass of water and, with nonchalance, balance it on the edge of its base (Fig. 15). After a minute or so, set it back on its base. The audience can now examine the glass and the tabletop for clues to the secret of this wonderful feat of juggling. Even if they look under the tablecloth, they will find nothing.

Fig. 15.

"All right, Mr. Magician, the glass has been on edge for over five minutes. When are you going to show us something else?"

Materials Needed

One half-filled heavy water glass
A one-inch piece of matchstick
A long piece of strong black thread

Preparation

The secret lies in the matchstick. Beforehand, tie the end of the thread around the middle of the matchstick (Fig. 16). Place the matchstick under the tablecloth in front of your place at the dinner table. The end of the string should hang down a couple of inches below the edge of the tablecloth. Since there is always the chance of someone trying this trick after you have presented it, and spilling water all over the table, it's best to present this stunt in your own home.

Fig. 16.

Presentation

The matchstick is small and will not be noticed in the folds and creases of the tablecloth. Wait until dessert and coffee to present this juggling sensation. Without mentioning what you're doing, take the glass and place it down so that its edge is resting on the wooden match. Now, adjust it until it's well balanced (Fig. 17). By this time your fellow diners will see what you are doing, and you will amaze them with this glass-balancing feat.

When it comes time to right the glass, reach out with your right hand to grasp it. Your left hand should be below the table, holding the end of the black thread. When you grip the glass, raise it up slightly and move it forward so that your hand covers the spot where the matchstick is positioned beneath the tablecloth.

While everyone's attention is on the glass, pull the match-

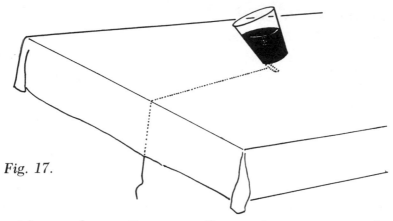

Fig. 17.

stick towards you. Your arm will cover the movement under the cloth. Keep pulling on the thread until the matchstick is in your left hand. It is now safe to let your audience examine the glass and the tablecloth.

A slightly more elaborate method of doing this trick is to have a secret assistant at the table pull the thread for you. In this case, you can have both hands plainly in sight during the entire performance. It would be best if your accomplice were sitting directly across the table from you.

THE GREAT RIBBON-AND-RING MYSTERY

Effect

Form a loop in the center of a length of ribbon and secure it with a safety pin. Then borrow a ring from someone and state that you will cause the ring to be placed on the loop without threading it through either end of the ribbon. Cover the loop and ring with a handkerchief, put your hands under the cloth, and seconds later remove the handkerchief, showing that the ring has become threaded on the center of the ribbon.

Materials Needed

One three-foot length of colored half-inch-wide ribbon
A large safety pin
A handkerchief
A finger ring

Presentation

Form a loop in the center of the ribbon and fasten it with a stout safety pin. Then place the borrowed finger ring next to it (Fig. 18). Next, place a handkerchief over the loop and ring and reach under it with both hands. With your hands under the cloth, remove the safety pin, take the end of the loop, and thread it through the ring (Fig. 19). This forms two loops in the ribbon, one facing up and one facing down. Now, take the safety pin and fasten it through the two sides of the "down" loop on the left of the ring (Fig. 20).

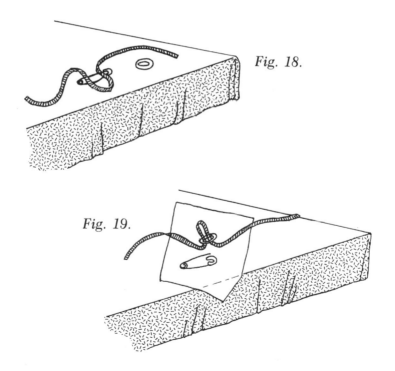

Fig. 18.

Fig. 19.

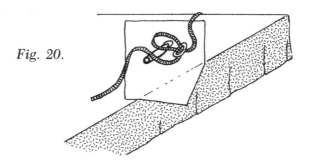

Fig. 20.

Next, hook the little finger of your right hand through the "up" loop on the right side. Grip the handkerchief with the other fingers of your right hand (Fig. 21). Now move your left hand from under the cloth to the left end of the ribbon. While holding down the end of the ribbon with the fingers of your left hand, make a flat, swiping motion to the right with your right hand, dragging the handkerchief out along the ribbon until it is clear of the table. The ribbon is now open to view on the table, with the ring neatly threaded in the center and firmly secured by the safety pin (Fig. 22).

There are two important points to remember when presenting this trick. First, make sure that the ends of the ribbon are always in view on either side of the handkerchief. Tell your audience to watch the ends while your hands are under the cloth. Second, before removing the handkerchief from the ribbon, be sure that your left hand is holding down the left

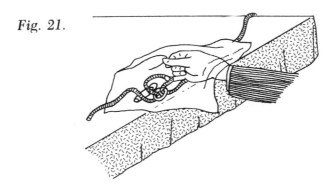

Fig. 21.

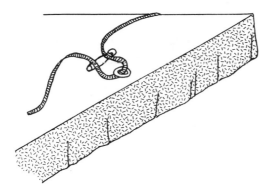

Fig. 22.

end of the ribbon firmly against the top of the table. If the end is not anchored, you will not be able to pull the loose end of the ribbon through the ring with the little finger of your right hand as you sweep the handkerchief to the right.

THE PENCIL-AND-STRING
PERPLEXITY

Effect

This is a clever trick that's sure to leave the audience perplexed. Show the audience a pencil that has a loop of string attached to it. Next, loop the pencil through the buttonhole in a spectator's shirt or coat. Once the pencil is in place, bet the spectator that he can't remove it in five minutes. Inform the spectator that he is not allowed to cut the string, break the pencil, or cut the buttonhole in attempting to win this bet.

Materials Needed

A stout piece of string about two feet long
A new pencil

Preparation

This is an easy magic trick to perform. It is also inexpensive, so have pencils made up with your name on them to give away for advertising.

To do the trick, you must first drill a hole in the pencil below the eraser. Then thread the piece of string through the hole and tie it so that when pulled tight the loop is about an inch from the end of the pencil (Fig. 23).

Fig. 23.

Presentation

To loop the pencil on a buttonhole, first place the fingers of your right hand through the loop in the string. Then, take hold of the buttonhole with your right hand and pull it and the cloth around it through the loop of string. Pull it far enough through the loop so that you can insert the end of the pencil through the buttonhole. Pull the pencil all the way through the buttonhole, and then pull the looped string tight (Figs. 24 and 25). Once you've done this, the trick is complete. Now the spectator has to try to escape from this diabolically clever contraption. Everyone will be amused watching him trying to solve this mystery.

The solution to this problem is to simply reverse the moves that you used to fasten the pencil on the coat. Open the loop shown in Fig. 25 and pass the eraser end of the pencil through it. When the pencil is halfway through, reach under it and take hold of the cloth by the edge of the buttonhole. Pull this cloth to the right while also pulling the pencil to the left. The pencil will come free of the loop, and you will then be able to release the loop from the buttonhole.

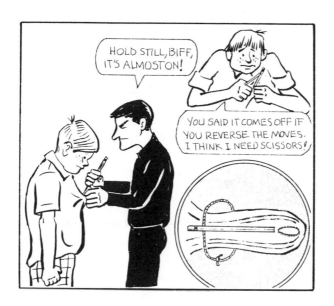

Fig. 24.

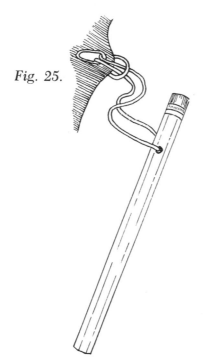

Fig. 25.

THE LEVITATING KNIFE

Effect

This is one of those delightfully entertaining impromptu effects that you can nonchalantly present between courses at your next dinner party. Interlock the fingers on both your hands and place them, palms down, on top of a dinner knife. When you raise your hands in front of you, the knife appears to be clinging to them.

At this point, both of your thumbs are hidden behind your fingers and everyone assumes that they are holding the knife against your palms. Tell them that this is not so, and raise your right thumb. They will say that your left thumb is now holding the knife. Move your right thumb back down behind your fingers and raise your left thumb. They will, of course, say that your right thumb is now holding the knife.

Repeat this back and forth several times, and then finally in exasperation raise both your thumbs to show them how wrong they are (Fig. 26). Shake your hands vigorously. The knife will still cling to them. Suddenly, pull your hands apart and let the knife fall to the table. Turn your hands palms up so that your dinner guests can see that they do not conceal anything that could have caused the knife to cling to them. How did you do it?

Presentation

The secret lies in the way you interlocked your fingers. Although no one is about to count your fingers, in reality only nine of them are showing (Fig. 26). When you interlock them, do it in such a way that the second finger of the right hand is curled into your palm (Fig. 27). When you pick up the knife, make sure that it goes under this finger, where it will be held in place until you unlock your fingers at the end of the trick.

This is a surprising trick, and one that you should have a lot of fun presenting.

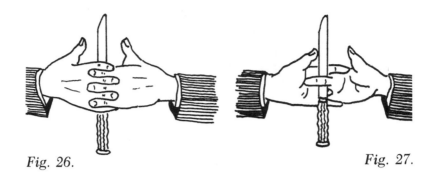

Fig. 26.   Fig. 27.

THE MIRACLE PREDICTION
• •

Effect

Place a stack of business cards on the table. The stack should contain about 20 cards and be fastened with a wide rubber band. Explain that the business cards once belonged to a famous medium by the name of Voltar, who had passed away, and that you had come across them at an estate sale last year. After reading the instructions that came with the cards, you realized that they contained a strange power that enabled Voltar to communicate from the other side. To prove this, you would like to try an experiment. Push the stack of cards forward and ask someone to write his, or her, initials in the rectangular box at the top of the card. Then remove this card from the stack and place it face down on the table.

Next, hand the person who initialed the card a pad of paper and request that he write down a number comprised of three different digits. The number must be between one hundred and one thousand. As an example, let's say that your assistant writes down the number 732 (Fig. 28). He is told to then reverse the number and subtract the smaller number from the larger number. The answer in our example is 495. If the answer had been a two-digit number, your assistant would have

Fig. 28.

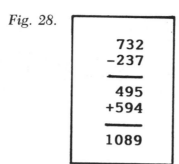

been told to place a zero in front of it so that there will be a three-digit answer.

Finally, tell your assistant to once again reverse this number, write the reversed number below the previous answer, and then add the two numbers together. In our example the final total is 1089.

Then stretch out your hands and tell the audience that it is now time to summon the Great Voltar. Everyone is to hold hands and chant the name Voltar three times. When this is done, tell your assistant to turn over the card he initialed and see if Voltar has come through. Sure enough, when he turns it over, he will find that the number 1089 is written in red in the scroll at the bottom of the card, thus proving that there is indeed magic after death (Fig. 29).

Materials Needed

The Voltar deck of cards as described in the
    Preparation section
A pad and a pencil

Preparation

The first thing that you will need to do is to make up 40 or 50 Voltar cards. The best, and cheapest, way to do this is to take the picture of the card shown in Fig. 30 and bring it to your local stationery store, where they can have a rubber stamp of it made up. Once you have the stamp, you can make as many cards as needed.

Fig. 29.

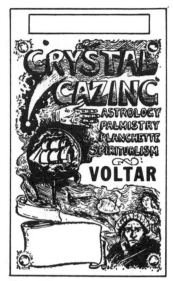

Fig. 30.

Next, you'll need several sheets of white business-card paper, which you can also get at a stationery store. After you've made up your cards, make a stack of 20 of them. Write the number 1089, in red, in the empty scroll at the bottom of the top card.

Next, take one of the cards and cut it in two. Place the bottom half of the card on top of the stack and fasten them together with a wide rubber band (Fig. 31). The rubber band should be at least a quarter of an inch wide. You're now ready to perform this trick.

Presentation

By this time you're familiar with both the presentation of this trick and the subtle method used to reveal the answer. The number 1089 is, of course, always the right answer, no matter what three-digit number your assistant chooses. Remember, though, that the three digits that make up the number must always be different. Numbers such as 333 or 101 will not work.

The critical move in working this trick is the removal of the card from the stack in such a manner that no one sees that the number is already written on it. The bottom half of this card is

Fig. 31.

covered by the half-card above it (Fig. 31). When you place the stack in front of your assistant to be initialed (Fig. 32), the pack does *not* look like it was tampered with (Fig. 33). After the top card has been initialed, take hold of its top edge and bend it away from the deck (Fig. 34). As you do this, start to rotate the deck away from the audience with your left hand. You should start to slide the card out from under the half-card and the rubber band with your right hand (Fig. 35). Both hands continue rotating towards your side of the table until the deck, and the top card, are turned upside down and are almost touching the table. Now draw the top card completely away from the deck with your right hand and place it face-down on the table (Fig. 36). This whole operation is done in one continuous movement and completely masks the card from view.

The mechanics of the trick are now complete. It's now up to you to embellish the revelation of Voltar's otherworldly powers. This is an extremely effective method of revealing things supposedly selected freely by a member of the audience.

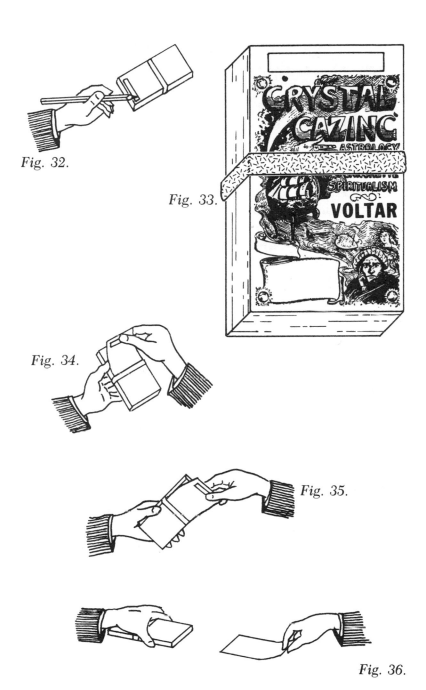

Fig. 32.

Fig. 33.

Fig. 34.

Fig. 35.

Fig. 36.

THE DOMINO MYSTERY

Effect

Dump a box of dominoes and a sealed envelope on the table. Then instruct two members of the audience to set up the dominoes in a long line on the table, matching the ends of each domino as you would when playing a game. When they're finished, explain to them that prior to today's performance you had a mental picture of a long line of dominoes and that you jotted down the numbers on the two end dominoes and placed this information in the envelope that is on the table. When they open up the envelope and read the paper, it says: "The number at one end of the line of dominoes is four, and the number at the other end is two."

Materials Needed

Dominoes
An envelope

Preparation

Before showing this trick, you must remove the four-two dominoes from the box and write the above note.

Presentation

If you were to lay out a complete set of dominoes in a circle, they would match where the two ends came together. Thus, if you remove any domino from the box and then lay them out in a straight line, the two end dominoes will always match the two numbers on the domino that you removed. Make sure that when you dump the box of dominoes on the table, no one sees that there is one missing when they're still in the box.

Card Magic

A CRAFTY CARD BET

Effect

Choose a member of the audience and play the following simple game with him: Take a deck of cards and spread it out on the table facedown. Then each of you should take turns turning over the cards. Whoever turns over the ace-of-spades is the loser. Needless to say, you will emerge the winner every time.

Presentation

Here's how it's done: Fifty percent of the time, the participant will turn the ace-of-spades over, making you the winner. However, whenever it's your turn to turn over a card, always turn up a corner of the card first, look at it, and then turn it over. If, when you do this, you see that the card is the ace-of-spades, turn the corner down and pick up some other card and turn it over. Make sure that your opponent sees you do this. He is then sure to say that you're cheating and reach over and turn the card over, thus losing the bet. Remember, the bet is that the first person to turn the ace-of-spades over is the loser.

THE ROYAL CARD TRICK

This is more of a puzzle than a trick, but I think that you'll enjoy fooling your friends with it. Place the 12 face cards and the 4 aces from the deck on the table and set the rest of the pack aside. Challenge your audience to arrange these 16 cards into 4 rows of 4 cards each in such a way that no horizontal row or vertical column shall contain 2 cards of the same suit or face value.

This problem was presented over one hundred and ten years ago by Professor Hoffmann in his famous book, *Modern Magic*. It's still a great puzzle. Fig. 37 shows the original solution that appeared in that magnificent collection of magic. The card faces have changed over the years, but I'm sure that you will have no trouble understanding the solution. The two diagonals should each contain 4 cards of the same value. In the solution, kings and aces are used. Whichever cards you use, make sure that the four cards that take up the center of the square represent the four suits: hearts, clubs, spades, and diamonds. Once these cards are in place, the rest should be simple for you to work out.

Fig. 37.

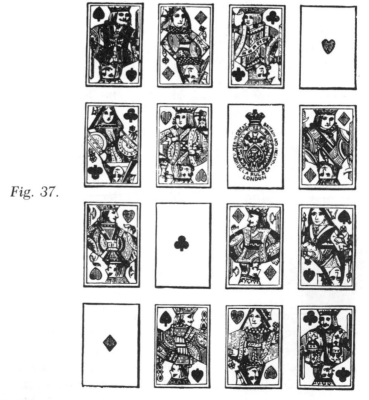

THE GREAT CARD-STABBING MYSTERY

....

Effect

A member of the audience selects a card from a shuffled deck, notes it, and returns it to the deck. He is then instructed to shuffle the deck and spread the cards out on the table. He is to thoroughly mix the cards about on the table. This is all done while you, the magician, have your back turned.

Next, lay a sheet of newspaper over the top of the table, covering all of the cards. Pick up a long dagger and wave it mysteriously over the newspaper much in the way a water diviner controls the forked divining rod when dowsing for water. After a few moments, plunge the dagger through the paper and stick it firmly into the table. Then tear away the newspaper around the dagger and pull the dagger out of the table. The card that is impaled on its point is of course the selected card.

Materials Needed

Two copies of the same page spread from the classified section
    of the newspaper
Rubber cement
Two similar decks of cards with the same color backing
A sheet of quarter-inch plywood the same size as the tabletop
An ornamental knife or dagger

Preparation

Remove the six-of-diamonds from one of the decks and put the deck aside. Next, cut out a five-inch square of newspaper from one of the pages, slightly left of center, and glue it over the same section of the other copy of the newspaper page. Just before you glue the piece down, place the six-of-diamonds under it. When gluing the piece of paper make sure that all of the print lines up evenly and that all the telltale edges are glued. Make sure that the card is faceup when you glue the paper over it.

Remember that you are only gluing down the edges of the square. Do not get any glue on the card. If done correctly, no one should be able to tell that the newspaper page contains a secret pocket with a card inside it (Fig. 38).

Place the plywood on the table. Take the second deck of cards, find the six-of-diamonds, and place it on top of the deck.

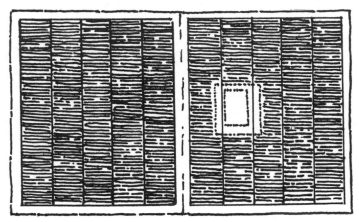

Fig. 38.

Presentation

In performing this trick the first thing you have to do is to manipulate your assistant into selecting the six-of-diamonds from your deck. Here is how to do it: While shuffling the deck, ask someone to step forward. Make sure that the six-of-diamonds stays on the top of the deck while you shuffle it. Place the deck on the table and ask the spectator to cut the deck.

After the spectator has cut the deck, hand him the dagger to examine (Fig. 39). As you hand him the dagger, pick up the bottom half of the deck and place it crosswise on top of the top half, saying that you will mark the cut while he looks at the dagger (Fig. 40). Chat with him for a few seconds, and then

Fig. 39.

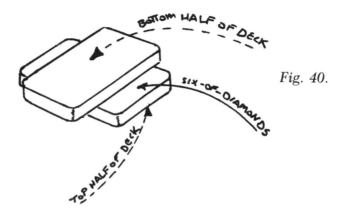

Fig. 40.

reach over and pick up the bottom half again. Tell your assistant to look at the top card of the pack on the table by saying, "Now, look at the card that you cut to, remember it, and replace it back on the deck."

Hand him the part of the deck that you are holding and tell him to shuffle the pack thoroughly while your back is turned, and then to spread the cards out over the table. When this is done, turn around, pick up the newspaper, and place it over the cards. You must put the side with the glued square face-down. When you prepare the newspaper, you will, of course, note what is opposite the pocket on the other side of the paper.

Now, pick up the dagger, wave it around, and finally drive it into the newspaper at the spot where the card is hidden in the paper pocket. Have your assistant lean on the knife while you tear away the newspaper. If the knife has been driven through more than one card, the top card will of course be the six-of-diamonds. Make sure that this is the card that remains stuck to the dagger as you work it free from the tabletop on the off chance that the other card under it may be the duplicate six-of-diamonds.

Ask your assistant to name his "chosen" card, and then show it stuck to the dagger point. A round of applause is sure to follow.

THE IN-THE-DARK POKER DEAL

Effect

Here's a good close-up trick with cards that you can perform when sitting at a table with three or four people. Take a card case out of your pocket and remove the cards from it. Hand the deck to someone and ask him to shuffle it. When he's finished, have him place it on the table in front of you.

Tell the people around you that you're going to deal out poker hands to everyone at the table, and to make sure that everything will be aboveboard you're going to deal in the dark. To do this, take a sheet of newspaper and place it over the deck of cards on the table. Then reach under the paper, pick up the deck, and deal out hands for everyone. When you're done, remove the newspaper, and instruct everyone to pick up his hand. The other players can discard and draw new cards as they would in a regular poker game. You should remain pat. When the hand is over, you will, of course, be the winner with a Royal Flush in spades.

Materials Needed

One deck of cards

Preparation

Before sitting down to play, secretly remove the ace-, king-, queen-, jack-, and ten-of-spades and slip them under the band of your wristwatch. Use your sleeve to cover up the cards. A sweater is even better, since the tight cuffs will effectively hold the cards in. Place the remainder of the deck in the box. You are now ready to amaze your friends.

Presentation

There's not much to add to the above description. The only moves you have to make are when you put your hands under the newspaper, at which point you pick up the deck and deal out the hands to the other players. When you're finished doing this, place the deck on the table and slip the cards out of your sleeve and place them in front of yourself. You now have only to remove the newspaper and proceed with the hand.

The beauty of the trick is that when it's all over there is a complete deck on the table that can be examined, leaving no one the wiser.

THE IN-YOUR-HAT CARD TRICK

Effect

This is one of those puzzle/tricks that every magician should use when a deck of cards is handy. Comment on the fact that oftentimes in life the simplest things are often the hardest to accomplish. To illustrate, place a felt or straw hat, crown down, on the floor and bet anyone present that you can drop more cards into the hat from a height of four feet than they can.

Materials Needed

One deck of playing cards
A felt or straw hat

Presentation

Look at the audience and say, "There is a knack to everything in life. Why, even something as simple as dropping cards into a hat can prove to be a tricky undertaking."

Place the hat, crown down, on the floor and stand in front of it. Take a card from the deck, and, holding it chest high above the center of the hat, comment, "Let's try an experiment.

Holding the cards four feet above the hat, we will release the cards one by one and see how many we can get to fall into the hat, or at least stay on the brim. To make it interesting, the person who gets the most cards in, or on, the hat will get ten cents a card from the loser." To illustrate, drop the card you are holding. (Figs. 41 and 42.) Give half the deck to the person who takes your bet and have him go first.

Fig. 41. Fig. 42.

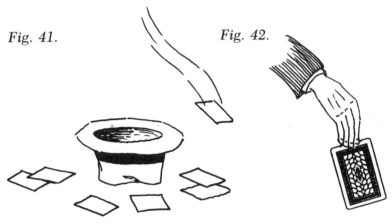

Since most people will hold the card by the end, as you demonstrated, most of their cards will miss the hat, sailing in all directions as they fall. When your opponent has finished, step up to the hat and show him how it's done. The secret to success is simple. Hold the card flat, gripping the sides with your thumb and fingers as shown in Fig. 43. When you release the card, it will fall straight down. With a little practice you should be able to hit the target at least nine out of ten times.

Fig. 43.

THE DO-AS-I-DO CARD TRICK

Here's an excellent card trick that will leave your audience guessing. Have someone from the audience come forward to assist you. When you're both seated, place two decks on the table and say:

"Thank you for coming forward. Here are two fresh decks of playing cards. Please take either one. Now then, follow me closely and do as I do. First, shuffle your deck and hand it to me. I'll do the same with the other deck and hand it to you.

"Next, place the deck I gave you on the table in front of you, and cut it into three piles going left-to-right. Now, look at the top card of the middle pile, note it, and place it back on top of the pile. I will do the same with my deck. Finally, we put our decks back together, square them up, and exchange them once again.

"Now, shuffle your deck and I will shuffle mine. Good. Now, look through your deck and find the card that you looked at before and place it facedown on the table. I will do the same and place my chosen card next to yours.

"All right now, on the count of three we'll turn the cards over. One, two, three! My word, they're both the same. Do you realize that the odds of that happening are over 2700 to 1? Yet every time I do this trick the cards always match. Truly amazing!"

Presentation

The explanation for this trick is simplicity itself. In the beginning when you shuffle and exchange decks with your assistant, note the bottom card of your deck before passing it along to him. When you cut your deck, cut it left to right. Tell your assistant to do the same to his deck. After he has looked at the middle card and placed it back on top, reach across and re-stack the piles for him, once again moving left to right. This puts the stack, whose bottom card you know, on top of the card that he has just looked at. Then tell the participant to restack the deck in front of you in the same way. After that, exchange decks and shuffle them. When you shuffle your deck, merely cut it three or four times; this does not alter the arrangement of the cards. Both of you now look through your decks for the chosen cards. Merely look through your deck until you come to the bottom card you noted at the beginning of the trick. The next card down will be the card that the participant chose. Now, wasn't that an easy trick?

THE GAMBLER'S DELIGHT

Effect

Recite the following story about a gambler of the Old West named One-Eye Swensen: One day One-Eye Swensen sat in on a poker game with Big Nose Carrie, Slow Draw Callahan, the Sagebrush Kid, and Cattle Annie. One-Eye dealt a game he called Cactus Poker. He dealt everyone five cards; the one with the highest hand won the pot. This, of course, was One-Eye. He then discarded the winning hand, gathered up the four losing hands, and dealt out four new poker hands, leaving out Cattle Annie.

Once again, when One-Eye turned over the cards he had the winning hand. He then threw away the winning hand, gathered up the three losing hands, and dealt out three new hands, this time leaving out the Sagebrush Kid.

You guessed it. One-Eye won a third straight time, beating out the competition with four aces. Needless to say, everyone went for their guns after that one, and how it all ended is anybody's guess. But how did One-Eye manage to win three straight hands? The answer is given below.

Materials Needed

One deck of cards

Preparation

Prior to presenting this poker trick, the performer must set up the deck. That is, the top 24 cards have to be arranged in a certain order. The setup, from the top card down, is: 5H, 9C, AH, 3D, 8D, 7D, AC, 5S, 9D, 8S, 9S, 6D, JH, AD, 8H, 5C, 9H, 5D, 10D, 8C, JD, AS, JC, and 4D (H = hearts; C = clubs; S = spades; D = diamonds).

Presentation

Pretend to shuffle the cards, but do not disturb the top 24 cards. As you start the story, deal out 5 poker hands facedown on the table and place the deck aside. Deal one card at a time to each of the hands; deal your hand last. Turn over each of the other four hands; then turn over the dealer's hand, showing that the 4 eights in it easily win the pot.

Next, turn each of the other hands facedown and discard the dealer's winning hand. Without disturbing the order of the cards in the remaining hands, gather them up as follows: Pick up the cards for the first hand on your left and place them on top of the second hand, then place these ten cards on top of the third hand, and finally place this stack on top of the fourth hand.

Mention that Cattle Annie had to drop out and deal four new poker hands on the table. Turn over the players' hands, and then show that once again the dealer has won with a straight flush.

Once again, turn the hands facedown, discard the dealer's winning hand, and stack the cards left to right as you did before. With the remaining 15 cards, deal out the last three poker hands. Turn over the two players' hands and then show them that One-Eye has the winning edge with four aces.

This is a nice trick that works itself, so you can concentrate on presenting your tale of gold and guns.

THE FAMOUS SPELLING-BEE CARD PUZZLE

$\cdot\cdot\cdot\cdot\cdot\cdot\cdot\cdot\cdot\cdot\cdot\cdot\cdot\cdot\cdot\cdot\cdot\cdot\cdot\cdot\cdot\cdot\cdot\cdot\cdot\cdot\cdot\cdot\cdot\cdot\cdot\cdot\cdot\cdot\cdot\cdot\cdot\cdot\cdot\cdot\cdot\cdot\cdot\cdot\cdot\cdot\cdot\cdot$

Effect

Here is another amazing card-setup trick. After shuffling the cards, take the top 13 cards from the pack and place the rest of the deck aside. Turn the cards faceup and spread them so that everyone can see that they are all different. State that these are the smartest cards in the deck, and to prove it you are going to conduct a spelling bee.

Close the packet up and turn it facedown in your left hand. Then say, "I'm going to spell out the name of each card in turn. For each letter named I will transfer one card from the top of the pack to the bottom. When the name is complete, the next card should be the one so named. Let's see if the cards are up to snuff today. A-C-E. Now we turn over the next card and yes . . . it's an ace. We'll put it aside and try the next one. T-W-O. And the next card is . . . a two. Two for two so far."

Carry on in this manner until all 13 cards have been spelled out.

Materials Needed

One deck of cards

Preparation

Remove and arrange 13 cards in the following setup, top card down: three, eight, seven, ace, queen, six, four, two, jack, king, ten, nine, and five.

Presentation

The trick works itself. To start, pretend to shuffle the cards, but make sure that the top 13 cards are undisturbed. Remove the top cards as a group and fan them so that your audience can see their faces. When you spell out each card, do it as follows: Let's say that you are spelling the word ACE. Spell A, remove the top card and place it on the bottom. Then spell C, remove the top card, and place it on the bottom. Next, spell E, remove the top card, and place it on the bottom. Then turn over the next top card, show that it is an ace, and place it aside. Continue in this manner until you reach the king, which you merely turn over and place on the table.

Your audience will quickly realize that the cards must have been set up beforehand, but this only adds to the mystery—and you can treat it as a puzzle for them to try to figure out.

THE ACES-AND-KINGS REVELATION

Effect

Here's an interesting variation of the famous Four Aces trick. Shuffle a pack of cards and place it in front of a member of the audience. Request that he cut the pack in half, putting the top half next to the bottom half (Fig. 44). In Fig. 44, the top half is numbered 3 and the bottom half 4.

Fig. 44.   **AUDIENCE**

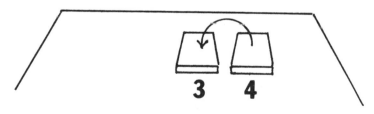

PERFORMER

Next, tell the spectator to cut the bottom half (labelled as 4) in half and to place it to the right of pile 3. This pile will be known as pile 2. Last, have him cut the top half (labelled as 3) in half and place it to the right of pile 2 (Fig. 45). This pile will be known as pile 1. When you instruct him to do all of this cutting, merely point to the pile and tell him to cut it and point to where he is to place the cut half.

Now give your assistant a series of instructions to move certain cards around:

1. Take the top card from pile 4 and place it on pile 3.
2. Take the top card from pile 2 and place it on pile 4.
3. Take the top card from pile 1 and place it on pile 2.
4. Take the top card from pile 3 and place it on pile 4.
5. Take the top card from pile 2 and place it on pile 4.
6. Take the top card from pile 1 and place it on pile 3.
7. Take the top card from pile 1 and place it on pile 2.

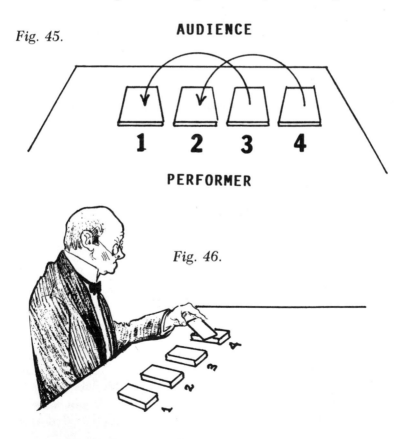

Fig. 45.

Fig. 46.

Stop for a moment and remind your assistant that he randomly cut the deck into four piles and what he is about to see is truly amazing. Instruct him to turn over the top card on each pile, where he will find all four aces.

"That's certainly an interesting surprise," you remark, "but we have more to come." Have him put the aces to one side and once again go through the above seven steps, moving the top cards of the piles around as he did before. This time, when he is finished, he will find that the top cards on the four piles are all kings.

Materials Needed
One deck of cards

Preparation
On top of the deck, place the four aces and the four kings. The aces should be on top of the kings.

Presentation
Shuffle the deck quickly a couple of times, but make sure that the top eight cards are not disturbed. Place the deck in front of your assistant and you are ready to proceed. Just follow the instructions as they are given in the **Effect** section and the trick will work itself.

After the deck was divided into four piles, all of the aces and kings were on top of pile number 1. Moving the top cards around helps to mask the distribution of the aces and kings.

THE ART OF CARD THROWING
• •

Effect
One of the oldest sleights in magic is card throwing. The great American magician Howard Thurston was reputed to have been able to sail cards from the street to the roofs of four-story buildings. When performing on a stage you can show your

ability in this art by throwing cards out to the audience. It's a pretty flourish with which to end a sequence of card tricks.

Materials Needed
One deck of cards

Presentation
To explain this art to the reader, we call upon that famous nineteenth-century writer, Professor Hoffmann:

"To Throw A Card—This sleight belongs rather to the ornamental than to the practical part of conjuring, but it is by no means to be despised. It is a decided addition to a card trick for the performer to be able to say, 'You observe, ladies and gentlemen, that the cards I use are all of a perfectly ordinary character,' and by way of offering them for examination, to send half-a-dozen in succession flying into the remotest corners of the hall or theatre.

"The card should be held lightly between the first and second fingers, in the position shown in Fig. 47. The hand should be curved inward toward the wrist, and then straightened with a sudden jerk, the arm being at the same time shot sharply forward. The effect of this movement is that the card, as it leaves the hand, revolves in the plane of its surface in the direction indicated by the dotted line, and during the rest of its course maintains such revolution. This spinning motion gives the flight of the card a strength and directness which it would seem impossible to impart to so small and light an object.

Fig. 47.

"A skilled performer will propel cards in this way to a distance of sixty or eighty feet, each card travelling with the precision, and well-nigh the speed, of an arrow shot from a bow. The movement, though perfectly simple in theory, is by no means easy to acquire in practice. Indeed, we know of no sleight which, as a rule, gives more trouble at the outset; but, after a certain amount of labour with little or no result, the student suddenly acquires the desired knack, and thence forward finds no difficulty in the matter." Professor Hoffmann wrote these words over 100 years ago in his monumental book, *Modern Magic*.

A second way, preferred by your author, is to hold the card as shown in Fig. 48.

Fig. 48.

Parlor Magic

THE SERFS-AND-SHEEP MYSTERY

Effect and Presentation

Here's an entertaining old trick about two hungry serfs and a barn full of sheep. According to the story, in the days of Robin Hood two hungry serfs wandered onto the estate of the Sheriff of Nottingham. (Use two hats to represent the Sheriff's two barns, five walnuts to represent the five sheep that they found grazing between them, and two other walnuts to represent

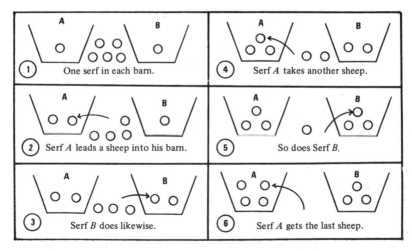

Fig. 49.

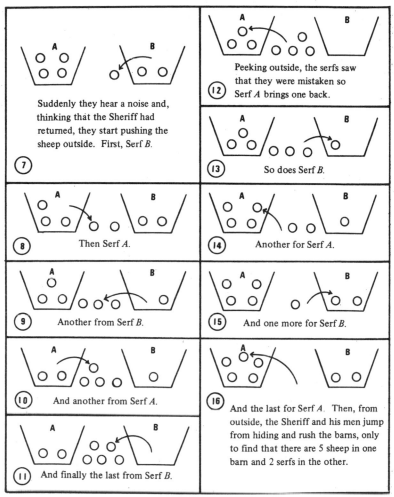

7 Suddenly they hear a noise and, thinking that the Sheriff had returned, they start pushing the sheep outside. First, Serf *B*.

8 Then Serf *A*.

9 Another from Serf *B*.

10 And another from Serf *A*.

11 And finally the last from Serf *B*.

12 Peeking outside, the serfs saw that they were mistaken so Serf *A* brings one back.

13 So does Serf *B*.

14 Another for Serf *A*.

15 And one more for Serf *B*.

16 And the last for Serf *A*. Then, from outside, the Sheriff and his men jump from hiding and rush the barns, only to find that there are 5 sheep in one barn and 2 serfs in the other.

Fig. 50.

the two serfs.) The desperate men decided to steal the five sheep and kill them in the barns. Each serf selected a barn. (Place one walnut into each hat.) Figs. 49 and 50 show how the story unfolds and the surprise ending. During each of the 16 moves shown, one walnut is either placed in a hat or is removed from a hat, to represent the action taking place.

A MIND-OVER-MATTER MYSTERY

Effect

This trick packs the punch of a stage illusion. Your presentation goes as follows:

"My next experiment is designed to show you not how much magical power I possess, but just how much *you* possess. Over here on this table we have a large wooden box. The front and back panels are hinged to the sides of the box. First, I open the front panel, and then the back panel, which allows us to see completely through the box (Fig. 51). In the box, I now place this large transparent glass vase. On the floor of the box, next to the vase, I place this round, cotton ball (Fig. 52).

"The stage is now set for you, the audience, to prove that the collective powers of your minds can move mountains, or, in this case, at least one cotton ball. I want all of you, at my command, to concentrate, with all of your energies, on causing that cotton ball to rise slowly up into the air, to drift over the vase, and finally, to descend into the vase and come to rest at the bottom. Since experience has shown that this can only be done if the concentrating minds cannot see the objects

Fig. 51.

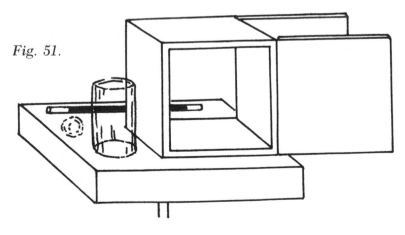

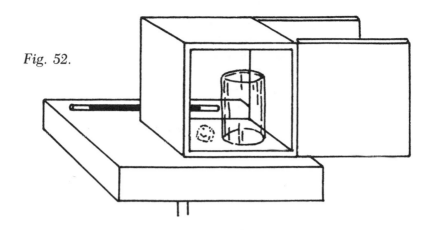

Fig. 52.

involved in the experiment, I will first close and latch the back panel, and then close and latch the front panel. There, that's done.

"Now, all together, mentally command the ball to rise! Very good! Now, command it to drift over the vase! Finally, lower it gently into the vase! Very good, I think that you have done it. We will know in a moment, just as soon as I have opened the front panel. Yes, there it is, the cotton ball is resting at the bottom of the glass vase. Let me congratulate each and every one of you on a job well done."

Materials Needed

A wooden box
A needle
Black thread
A glass vase
A cotton ball
A magic wand

Presentation

And now for the explanation. Like so many other mysterious tricks of the magician's art, the key is a piece of very fine black thread. A small hole is drilled into the top of the box.

To set up the illusion, thread a needle with the black thread and pass the needle through the hole in the top of the box. Next, pass the needle back and forth several times through the cotton ball. Form a loop on the other end of the thread and slip it over one end of the magic wand. At the moment when you place the glass vase into the box, your setup should look like the setup shown in Fig. 53. The black thread will, of course, be invisible to your audience.

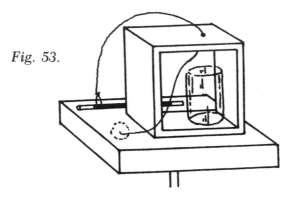

Fig. 53.

When the cotton ball has been placed in the box and the doors have been closed, pick up the wand and move away from the box. When you do this, the thread attached to the wand will pull the cotton ball up inside the box until it reaches the ceiling of the box (Fig. 54). The thread will then pull loose from the ball, and the ball will drop down into the vase.

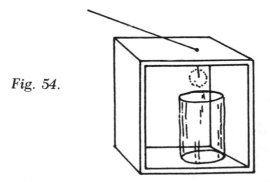

Fig. 54.

Make sure that the vase is placed directly under the hole in the top of the box. Paint the inside and outside of the box black. Paint the outer rim of the box and front and back panels white. Use a glass vase that has straight sides so that the cotton ball will not snag on the way up and pull loose from the thread prematurely. The vase should also be fairly tall and wide so that the cotton ball, once it is free from the thread, will fall down into the vase, not bounce off the rim and fall outside it.

The operating principle involved with this trick is a very good one and lends itself to subtle variations. Instead of attaching the thread to the wand, the thread can extend to another room and be operated by an unseen assistant. Instead of using doors, you might drape a small cloth over the front of the box. You might do away entirely with the box and use four tall Pilsner glasses at the corners with a wicker serving tray on top and a silk cloth in front. Use your imagination, and practice well before presenting the trick.'

A SPOOKY SÉANCE

Effect

State that you will give a spirit séance under the most rigid of conditions. Set up a card table a few feet from the audience and place a large cloth over it, one that will hang down to the floor on all sides. Next, place a wooden chair behind the table facing the audience. On the table place a slate, a bell, and several other objects for the spirits to play with.

Now, step forward and ask someone to act as your assistant. Tell your assistant to securely tie a rope around your left wrist and then tie another rope around your right wrist. Then fold your arms in front of yourself, turn around, and instruct your assistant to tie the ends of the two ropes tightly behind your back so that you cannot move your arms. Once this has been done, sit down on the wooden chair and instruct your assistant to tie the ends of the rope to the middle bar of the back of the chair. Also, instruct him or her to tie each of your legs to a leg of the chair.

Next, have him place a cardboard screen in front of the objects on the table. Although it is obvious that you cannot use your hands or feet and that the top of your head is visible at all times, the bell begins to ring, objects are thrown over the screen, and any number called for is written on the slate.

When the screen is removed, you will still be securely bound to the chair. How is a thing like this possible? Could you have had a hand in these actions? Definitely!

Materials Needed

Four six-foot lengths of rope

A card table

A slate

A bell

A wooden straight-back chair

A three-sided screen made of cardboard that can stand upright by itself on a card table. The screen must be high enough to conceal all but the top of the performer's head when he is seated behind the table.

A large cloth

Presentation

The secret, as in all good feats of magic, is simplicity itself. After the ropes have been tied to your wrists, start to fold your arms and turn your back so that the audience can see the ropes being tied behind you. While folding your arms, grasp the rope tied to your left wrist with your right hand and grasp the rope tied to your right wrist with your left hand (Fig. 55).

When you have completed the folding of your arms, it will appear from the back that each hand is holding the rope that is

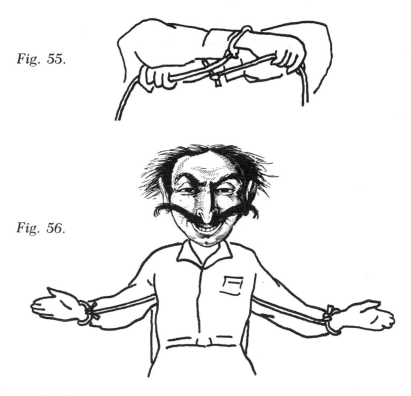

Fig. 55.

Fig. 56.

tied to that wrist. After the two ropes have been tied together, sit down and have the ends tied to the center bar at the back of the chair. Although you appear to be tied up, you can, in reality, unfold your arms and reach any item in front of you on the table (Fig. 56). The spirit manifestations that you perform I leave to your own imagination. The beauty of this trick is that it really looks as if you are tied up, and you would be if you had not reversed the ropes as you turned around.

Remember, the best feat of magic is simply a trick with showmanship added to entertain the audience. The key word here is "entertain." So, think before you act, and practice, practice, practice before you perform.

THE TOWNSEND ULTIMATE PRODUCTION BOX

....

Effect

Call the audience's attention to a simple wooden box standing on a bare table. The box is sitting on a small wooden stand. Open the front door of the box and show that the interior is empty. Close the door and turn the box completely around on the stand. Still nothing to be seen. Then open both the front and the back doors of the box, allowing the audience to see completely through. Once more, close the doors and revolve the box. The box is completely empty. Now open the top of the box and pull out a live rabbit. The Ultimate Production Box strikes again!

Materials Needed

Plywood
Screws
Glue
Paint
Hinges
Mirrors
Dowel rod
Felt
Hardware
Two magnetic door catches

Construction

This is the only trick in this book that really calls for the reader to exercise his construction skills. If you're not handy around the workshop, get someone to do most or all of the woodworking, and do painting and decorating yourself. The effort that you put into constructing this production box will be amply rewarded. Although the box makes use of two old and well-known magic tricks, namely the Mirror Box and the

Swing-Load Door, I have never seen both methods employed together before. You can't buy this box in the magic stores, so if you take the time to build it you'll possess a truly unique piece of equipment.

No dimensions are given with this description, as the size of the box will vary with the size of the production load. Fig. 57 shows the box mounted on the stand with the front door open. The box appears empty because the load is hidden behind two mirrors in the back half of the box that are set at a 45-degree angle. The inside sides of the box are painted with vertical stripes. When viewed from the front, the mirrors give the illusion that the two sides and the back of the box are painted with stripes. The floor and the top of the inside are painted with two diagonal stripes. These stripes hide the lines of the mirrors. Running through the center of the box is a pole, which the box revolves around.

FRONT VIEW

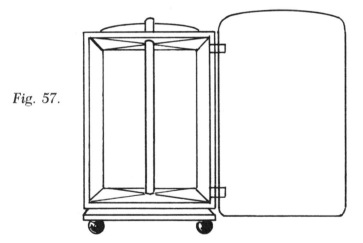

Fig. 57.

Fig. 58 shows the cabinet stand that the box sits on. The stand is raised above the table on four blocks, or feet. The floor of the stand is three-quarter-inch-thick plywood. Mounted on the center of the stand is a round three-quarter-inch-thick piece of plywood that serves as a spacer block. The top of the spacer is covered with black felt. The box sits on this

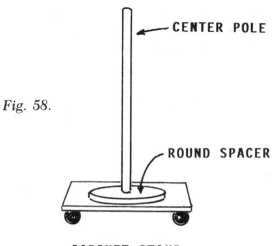

Fig. 58.

CABINET STAND

felt-covered spacer, which offers little resistance when the magician is revolving the box around the stand while showing the audience that it is empty.

Through the center of the stand is a one-inch-diameter wooden dowel rod. The cabinet has holes in the center of its top and bottom, and the entire box slides down over the dowel rod when sitting on the stand.

The secret load compartment that holds the items to be produced is attached to the back door of the box. Fig. 59 shows a view of the production box from the top when it is opened as shown in Fig. 62. The load chamber is triangular, with mirrors on its two front sides. When this door is closed, the point where the two mirrors meet is covered by the center pole of the stand. While both the front and back doors are as wide as the box, they are both longer than the height of the box. This is to prevent the audience from detecting the load chamber from the front of the box. When presenting this trick, make sure that the eye level of the audience is not above the top of the back door of the box.

Fig. 59 also shows the two doors at the top of the box. They open on either side of the center pole and have small brass knobs.

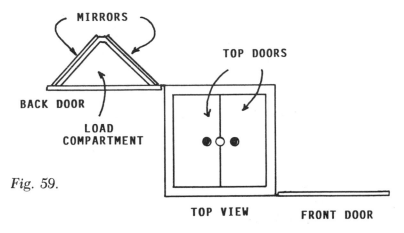

MIRRORS

TOP DOORS

BACK DOOR

LOAD COMPARTMENT

Fig. 59.

TOP VIEW   FRONT DOOR

Fig. 60 gives the reader a more detailed look at the load compartment on the back door.

Fig. 61 is a construction detail of the main part of the production box. It's made of three-quarter-inch-thick plywood. The boards are attached with countersunk wood screws. The holes are filled with plastic wood. Fill all holes in the edges of the plywood with plastic wood, and then sand and paint them.

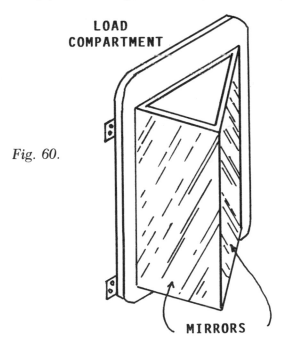

LOAD COMPARTMENT

Fig. 60.

MIRRORS

Fig. 61.

TOP DOORS

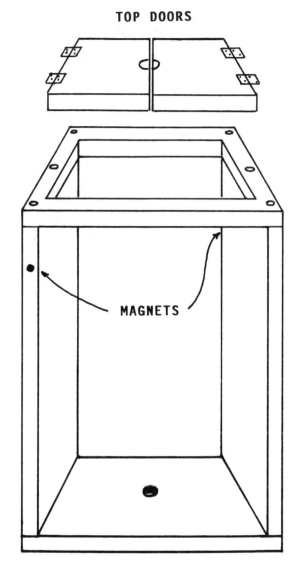

MAGNETS

CONSTRUCTION
DETAIL

Fig. 62.

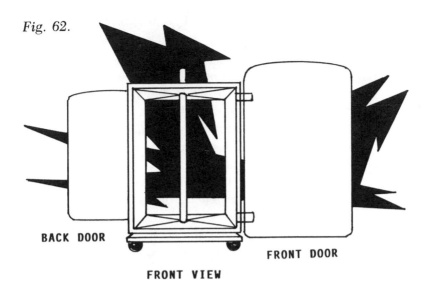

BACK DOOR

FRONT DOOR

FRONT VIEW

Fig. 63.

FRONT VIEW

Drill holes in the top and bottom boards slightly larger than the center pole of the stand. Carefully cut out the top doors, fill in their edges, and then sand and paint them. Attach the top doors with hinges to the top of the box.

Construct the front and rear doors, finish and paint them, and attach them to the box frame. The load chamber should be an eighth of an inch shorter than the inside height of the box, so that when you close the rear door it will easily slide in. This is the most delicate part of constructing the box. First, mount the rear door before attaching the load chamber to it. Close the door and, with a pencil, trace the inside of the cabinet frame onto the back door. Remove the door, place it on your workbench, and attach the load compartment to it (Fig. 60). Great care should be taken in building both the load chamber and making sure that the inside of the box is perfectly square. When closed, the load chamber should fit snugly in place behind the center pole. It also should be able to move in and out of the box without binding.

Build two magnetic latches into the side frames to keep the doors from swinging open when you are turning the box around for inspection. Drill a hole into the frames about four inches from the top, and insert a round magnet so that it is flush with the outside of the wood (Fig. 61). On the inside of the doors, opposite the magnets, inlay a small strip of metal. These magnetic latches will safely hold the doors shut.

When you paint the inside of the box, the two diagonal stripes on the bottom and top should be three-quarters of an inch in width. Paint all surfaces with a high-gloss enamel paint, for durability.

Presentation

By this time, the presentation of this trick should be pretty well established in your mind. Figs. 64–69 show how to manipulate the box.

Fig. 64 shows the box with its front door open and the load in place behind the center pole.

Fig. 65 shows the box with its front door closed. The magi-

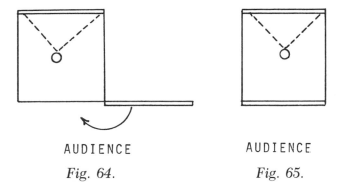

AUDIENCE

Fig. 64.

AUDIENCE

Fig. 65.

cian now turns the box slowly around so that the audience gets to see all sides of it.

Fig. 66 shows the box after you have finished turning it around. The back door is now facing the audience. The performer now takes hold of the back door with his right hand and the front door with his left hand and moves his hands apart. This causes the box to revolve in the direction indicated in Fig. 66.

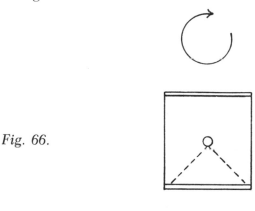

Fig. 66.

AUDIENCE

Fig. 67 shows the box after it has rotated 180 degrees. The front and back doors are both open, and the load chamber is hidden behind the back door (Fig. 62 shows the audience's view at this time). The magician gives the audience a moment

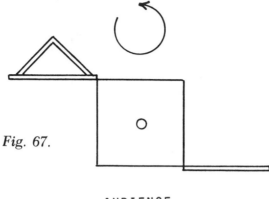

Fig. 67.

AUDIENCE

to look completely through the box. He is still holding the doors in his hands as before. He now reverses his previous movements and rotates the cabinet in the opposite direction 180 degrees.

Fig. 68 shows the box back at its previous position, with the back door towards the audience. The front door is still open at the back. The magician now continues to rotate the box another 180 degrees, ending up with the front of the box facing the audience and the front door still open. The audience is given a last look at the "empty" interior before the performer finally closes the door.

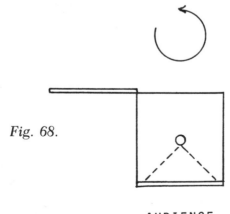

Fig. 68.

AUDIENCE

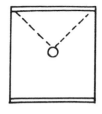

Fig. 69.

Fig. 69 shows the box just prior to the production of the rabbit. The performer now reaches down and opens the two doors on the top of the box, reaches in, and pulls out the trademark of his profession . . . a white, furry rabbit (Fig. 63).

Some last thoughts concerning the Ultimate Production Box: As I mentioned, there are no dimensions with the drawings given here. Construct a box to suit your production needs. If you are producing a rabbit, then the box should be just big enough to hold one. On the other hand, you may decide to produce something such as a tall, thin crystal vase half filled with water and with a red rose in it. This would call for a box of different proportions.

By this time, I think that you should understand the concept involved in using this production box. I wish you luck in your presentation of this trick. I would be interested in hearing from anyone who constructs and uses it.

PLATE JUGGLING

Effect

At the turn of the century, plates were a prominent entertainment item of stage and vaudeville performers. Jugglers and magicians made great use of them. In Fig. 70, a celestial entertainer is showing a 1910 audience his version of a flying saucer. More about this feat later.

Fig. 70.

Of more practical interest to the reader are two very interesting feats of juggling that can be used as a prelude to some other trick that makes use of a plate. The first trick deals with the dropping, and catching, of a plate just before it hits the floor. The second feat gives the illusion of a plate rapidly revolving between your two hands.

Materials Needed
One china dinner plate
One plastic dinner plate for practicing

Presentation
Both of these feats, or flourishes, were well documented by that most prolific of magic writers, Will Goldston, some 80 years ago. Since I could never improve on Mr. Goldston's description of the workings of these flourishes, I'm going to turn the stage over to him:

"An amusing little piece of byplay with a plate consists in dropping it and catching it—apparently without an effort—just before it touches the ground. The trick is very showy, but it is not at all difficult to master.

"Bend the right arm and, holding it close to the body, rest

the plate on the arm, just above the cuff [Fig. 71]. Now, if the arm is moved downwards the plate will fall, but the right hand will be exactly behind it [Fig. 72]. Extend the arm so that the right hand travels downwards behind the plate, the back of the hand being towards the back of the plate [Fig. 73]. When the plate has almost reached the ground, lift the right hand slightly, and the fingers will be in such a position that they can easily grasp the edge of the plate [Fig. 74].

Fig. 71.   Fig. 72.   Fig. 73.

Fig. 74.

"The performer appears to the audience to stoop down exactly at the critical moment and to take hold of the plate just before it touches the ground; another second, apparently, and he would have been too late. The audience does not realize that the performer's hand has travelled down behind the center of the plate, and that when he wants to grasp the plate, all he has to do is to lift his right hand a few inches. In other words, what the performer does is really much easier than the feat which the audience believes he performs.

"The second feat that I'm going to explain to you deals with handling a plate in such a manner that it appears to be revolving between your hands. When the trick is done smartly, the plate seems to be running round the hands. Of course, a good deal of practice will be required before this effect is produced, and the student should practice with a plastic plate unless he is content to go through all his rehearsals while standing over a bed.

"The directions for turning the plate must be followed very carefully, or it will be impossible to perform the feat with any certainty. The practice should be done very slowly at first, until the correct movements have been learned by heart and the student is not obliged to stop to look at the directions and the accompanying illustrations.

"The student begins by holding out his left hand with the palm uppermost and placing the plate on that hand [Fig. 75]. He then puts his right hand underneath the plate and on the side nearest to him and turns the plate by putting the little finger of the right hand against it. The plate thus turns on the left hand. When it is turned right round so that it is resting on the palm of the right hand, the left hand goes under it and turns it by raising it with the little finger. The plate thus turns on the right hand until it is brought back to the original position on the left hand, when the right hand at once begins its work once more.

"At first progress with this trick will be very slow, but with a little practice the feat will be made very effective. The great thing to remember is to raise the plate with the little fingers. The positions of the hands will seem unnatural at first, but if

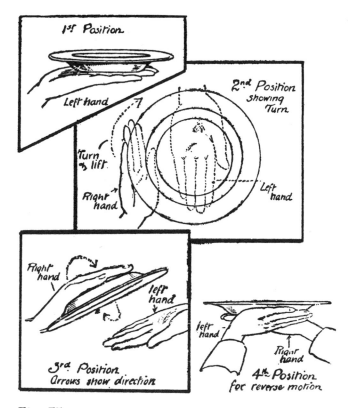

Fig. 75.

they are held in any other way the plate will probably fall."

Please give these tricks a try. You'll be surprised how quickly you'll become proficient at presenting them.

I doubt that any of my readers will have an opportunity to present this feat, but Fig. 76 shows how the feat was accomplished. First, a hole was bored in the center of the plate, and then the end of a stout piece of fishing line was threaded through it. A small button was attached to the line. The other end of the fishing line was attached to a three-foot length of elastic cord, which was, in turn, fastened to the ceiling of the playhouse. The elastic imparted a certain amount of play to the cord.

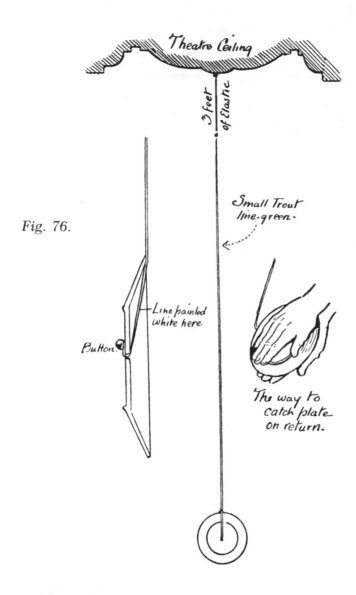

Fig. 76.

Theatre Ceiling

3 feet of Elastic

Small Trout line-green.

Line painted white here

Button.

The way to catch plate on return.

Now, all you have to do is send the plate spinning out in one direction and catch it on its return. In this day of excessive litigation, I would certainly shy away from sending a plate flying out over the heads of an audience. However, you might consider this alternative: Position your fishing line at a point directly over the center of the stage. Make a mark on the floor at this point. Now, if you stood on this mark and made a sweeping motion to the right with your fully extended arm just before you released the plate, it would describe a perfect circle about your body. You could then turn slightly to the left and be in position to catch the plate between your hands as it finishes the circle. Doing it this way would preclude the need to send the plate out over the audience. The fishing line should be dark. The house lights should be dim, and there should be a spotlight on you and the plate.

Mental Magic

A QUICK MATH MYSTERY

Effect

In passing, remark that you were born with an uncanny mathematical talent. For some reason, you are able to merely look at a number and tell if the number can be evenly divided by 4, no matter how many digits it contains. And if the number cannot be evenly divided by 4, you can figure out how to make it evenly divisible by adding one or two digits to it.

To illustrate your talent, invite someone to write down a random number of up to 20 digits. Let's assume he writes down the number 28450295812329104439392. Glance at the number for a second or two and declare that it cannot be evenly divided by 4, but that you'll fix it so that it can be. Then add the number 28 to the end of the number and instruct the person who wrote down the number to try dividing it by 4. Sure enough, after a minute of hard work, he will find that the number 2845029581232910443928 can indeed be evenly divided by 4. Chalk another one up for the Mental Wizard.

Presentation

The answer to this mystery is almost too simple. The truth is that any number that you add 28 to can be evenly divided by 4. A long number, with over 15 digits, helps to throw the spectators off the track. This trick is very effective, but don't repeat it or the method becomes obvious. Use the trick as an effective filler between two other larger, and more complicated, mental mysteries. Present it as a sort of afterthought, an interesting aside into the many avenues of your mental powers.

THE MAGIC MEMORY

Here's a mental mystery that will astound your friends. Make several photocopies of the card shown in Fig. 77 and mount them on fairly stiff cardboard. When you present this trick, pass the cards out and request that members of the audience

(23)	(39)	(18)	(22)	(4)	(38)
4370774	0550550	9213471	3369549	5167303	9437077
(2)	(45)	(30)	(34)	(25)	(6)
3145943	6516730	1459437	5493257	6392134	7189763
(9)	(37)	(46)	(3)	(1)	(17)
0224606	8426842	7527965	4156178	2134718	8202246
(21)	(5)	(44)	(11)	(41)	(19)
2358314	6178538	5505505	2246066	2572910	0336954
(29)	(12)	(33)	(13)	(43)	(7)
0448202	3257291	4482022	4268426	4594370	8190998

Fig. 77.

call out any of the two-digit numbers enclosed in parentheses. Immediately tell them what the seven-digit number below it is. You can do the whole card if they can stand it. The secret of your amazing memory is very simple. It goes like this:

A) Take the number they give you, say 25, and add 11 to it (giving us 36 for this example).

B) Reverse the result. This gives you the first two digits of your answer (63).

C) From this point on, always add the previous two numbers as you construct your number. The third digit will be 9 (6 plus 3 = 9).

D) For the fourth digit, add 3 and 9, getting 12. When the sum gives you a double-digit answer, drop the 10's position and use the unit's position. Our digit here is 2.

E) The fifth digit is 1 (9 plus 2 = 11, drop the 10's position, and use the unit's position, 1).

F) The sixth digit is 3 (2 plus 1 = 3).

G) The seventh and final digit is 4 (1 plus 3 = 4).

Our final answer for the number 25 is *6392134*.

With a little practice, you should be able to do all of these calculations in your head. When you're giving the answers, it's best to have a blackboard or large pad to write on so that your audience can see the number as you "recall" it. Also, writing down the number on a blackboard makes it easier for you to mentally generate it.

Now, go forth and mystify the world, O Mighty Master of Mathematical Marvels and Miscellaneous Meanderings.

A MENTAL CARD MYSTERY

Effect

Instruct a spectator to sit down at the table, and hand him a stack of nine cards. Say, "Here are nine cards from the deck, ace through nine. I want you to shuffle these cards, and when you're through, please deal them into three rows of three cards each [Fig. 78]. While you're doing this, I'm going to be seated over here with my back towards you."

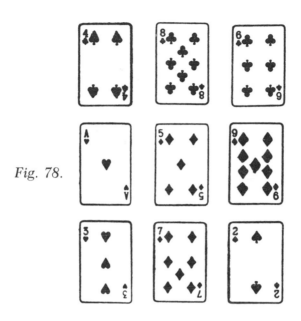

Fig. 78.

When the participant has finished dealing out the cards, tell him to remove any one of the cards, show it to the audience, and then place it in his pocket. When this is done, he is to add up the three rows of numbers represented by the cards. He is to consider the empty space from the card that he pocketed as a zero. In the example shown in Fig. 79, the total comes to 1,008.

Finally, the participant is instructed to add up all of the figures in the answer and to tell the performer what their sum is. In our example, the sum would be 9. The magician now, without turning around, states that the card that the spectator has chosen and pocketed is the 9 of diamonds. This is, of course, the right answer.

Fig. 79.

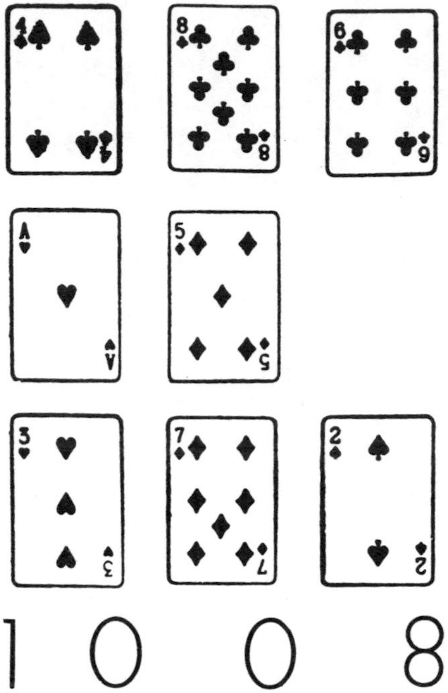

1 0 0 8

Materials Needed
One deck of cards

Presentation
This trick works every time. You can have the spectator re-place the card that he chose, rearrange the cards, and do it again and you will have no trouble in telling him what his new card is. All that you have to do is to take the number that he gives you and subtract it from 9 to get the value of the card. If the number is greater than 8, as in our example, simply sub-tract the number from 18 to get the card number. The suit of the card is calculated as follows:

1. The red cards are always odd, and the black cards are always even.
2. Numerically, the first two odd cards (ace and 3) are hearts.
3. Numerically, the next three odd cards (5, 7, and 9) are diamonds.

4. Numerically, the first two even cards (2 and 4) are spades.
5. Numerically, the next two even cards (6 and 8) are clubs.

With a little practice, you should have this trick down pat in no time.

A MENTAL PORTRAIT

· ·

Effect

Step forward holding a box containing several blank slips of paper and some pencils, and say: "My next experiment deals with the science of Mental Telepathy. I would like each person in the front row to take a blank slip of paper and a pencil from this box. Just pass the box down along the row.

"Now, I want each of you to think of some famous world leader of the past and write his or her name on the slip of paper. Write any name at all, you have thousands to choose from. Watch out, don't let your neighbor see what you are writing! Are you all finished? Fine, now fold your slips and place them in the box. Very good. Will the last person who placed his slip in the box please bring it forward to me? Thank you, sir. Now, please take the box and shake it vigorously back and forth so that the slips inside will be thoroughly mixed together. I can see that you are definitely a good mixer.

"Now, when I remove the lid I want you to reach in, take out one of the slips and move over to the other side of the room. Perfect. Now, please open the slip, read the name to yourself and then concentrate on sending me a mental picture of the person whose name appears on the slip. I will, in turn, attempt to draw a picture of this person on this large sketch pad. All right, start concentrating. Yes, that's very good; I can see the figure clearly . . . he was an American president . . . he wore glasses . . . I see a large mustache . . . I see a lot of teeth . . . yes, it is Teddy Roosevelt . . . am I right? Of course I'm right, I never fail!"

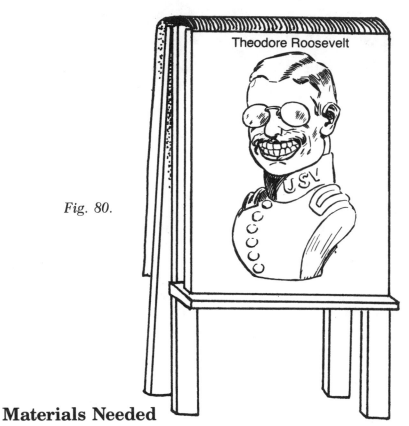

Fig. 80.

Materials Needed

A large candy box

Twelve or more blank pads of paper and the same number of short pencils

An easel

A large newsprint sketching pad

Preparation

The secret to this mystery lies in the box used to collect the slips in. Though it is just a large candy box, hidden in its lid is a smaller second box (Fig. 81). The deep sides of the lid hide this smaller box from view.

In the beginning, remove the lid and pass out the bottom of the box, which contains the pencils and slips of paper (Fig. 82). When everyone has taken a slip and a pencil, replace the

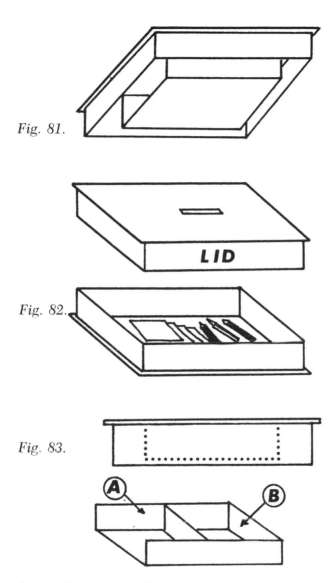

Fig. 81.

LID

Fig. 82.

Fig. 83.

A   B

lid on the box. At all times, make sure that no one is able to look inside the lid. The small box inside the lid (Fig. 83) is divided into two compartments. Compartment A is open at one end and is filled with twelve folded slips, each of which has the name of Teddy Roosevelt written on it. Compartment B is closed on all sides.

Presentation

Everything is done as described in the **Effect** section above. When the people in the front row push their folded slips into the top of the box, they all go into compartment *B* (Fig. 84). Now, when the gentleman comes forward with the box and shakes it back and forth, all of the slips in compartment *A* fall to the bottom of the box (Fig. 85). When he takes a slip out of the box, it has to be one with Teddy Roosevelt's name on it.

One thing that you must do when constructing the small inner box is to adhere it to the inside of the lid in such a way that you can easily remove it after every performance so that you can empty out compartment *B* and load a fresh batch of slips into compartment *A*.

You would be well advised to always use a different famous person's name each time you perform this trick so that any person witnessing it for a second time will have no clue as to your mode of operation. Practice making a rough sketch of the person whose name you are using. A few prominent features are all you will have to draw. At the conclusion of the trick, sign your masterpiece and give it to the person who assisted you as a souvenir.

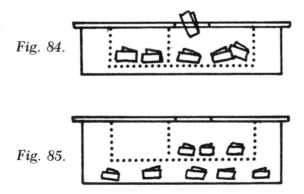

Fig. 84.

Fig. 85.

X-RAY VISION

Effect

In this trick, you, the magician or mentalist, work openly with an assistant. Claim that your assistant has the powers of a true medium and can perform many wondrous feats such as predicting the future, turning lead to gold, and actually being able to see through solid walls and other impenetrable objects. Tonight the two of you are going to give a small demonstration of this great power.

Ask the medium to leave the room with a member of the audience, to keep him under surveillance. Once they are out of the room, request the help of someone else from the audience. Instruct this person to take your deck of cards, shuffle it, and freely select any card he wishes from the deck. Tell the spectator to show the card to the rest of the audience. Then hand the spectator a sheet of aluminum foil and request that he wrap the card in it so that no portion of the card is visible. Next, give him an envelope and tell him to seal the card inside and to place the envelope in his coat pocket and wait for the medium to return.

Now state that you will leave the room before the medium is brought back to demonstrate his abilities. When the medium returns, he should stop and stare at the spectator with the envelope for several seconds, and then name the card.

Materials Needed

One deck of cards
A box with its roll of aluminum foil
An envelope

Presentation

Since you are not in the room when the medium returns, you must leave something there that will indicate to the medium what card the spectator has selected. It has to be something that will not arouse any suspicion among the audience. What you use is the box of aluminum foil on the table. As soon as the card is selected, you and the rest of the audience will know its identity. After you tear off a piece of foil to wrap the card in, place the foil box back on the table. Where, and how, you place it will signal to the medium the identity of the chosen card.

The table is mentally divided into twelve sections, each section representing a card value ranging from ace (as the lowest card) to queen (Fig. 86). Placing the box in any one of these sections will indicate its value. Placing the box anywhere on the table with any part of it sticking over the edge of the table will indicate that the card is a king.

Fig. 86.

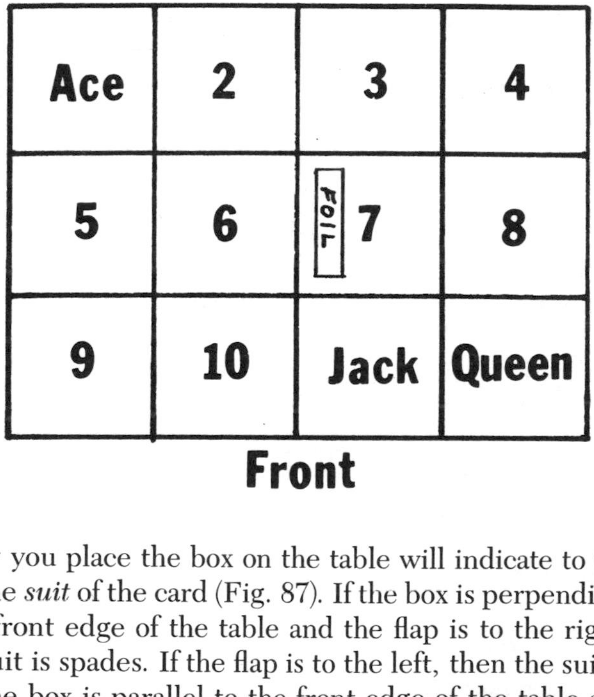

Ace	2	3	4
5	6	FOIL 7	8
9	10	Jack	Queen

Front

The way you place the box on the table will indicate to the medium the *suit* of the card (Fig. 87). If the box is perpendicular to the front edge of the table and the flap is to the right, then the suit is spades. If the flap is to the left, then the suit is clubs. If the box is parallel to the front edge of the table and the flap is to the front, then the suit is hearts. If the flap is to the back, then the suit is diamonds.

The beauty of using the box to convey the card's identity is the fact that it is on the table during your whole act. You only

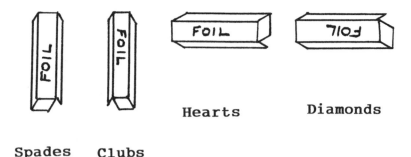

Hearts   Diamonds

Spades   Clubs

Fig. 87.

handle it briefly, and it supposedly has no relation to the trick being performed. With the right presentation, this can be a stellar effect in your act.

A MENTAL MAGIC SQUARE

Effect

Stand in front of the audience and say: "Magic Squares rank as one of the oldest mental amusements in history. In the past it took mathematicians days or even weeks to construct specific squares. In this age of computers it can be done somewhat quicker, but I have found that given the right training the human mind can do as well. To prove this point I am going to attempt to construct, in my head, a magic square comprised of 16 different numbers. Madam, will you give me a number between three and ten? Four will be fine. And you, sir, could I have a number between zero and ten? Seven, very good! I will now generate a magic square for you that will add up to 47 in each horizontal row, in each vertical column, and in each of the major diagonal lines. Quiet, please!

"Yes, I can see the answer now. The numbers are falling into place. I will now fill in the grid on this drawing pad with the finished magic square.

"There it is, folks, and, I've added a bonus! The four corner squares on each side, plus the four center squares, also add up to 47. That was exhausting. Please keep this drawing as a souvenir."

That's your presentation. Now we'll tell you how it's done.

Materials Needed

An easel
A large newsprint sketching pad
A large-tip black marking pen
A light-blue pencil
A ruler

Preparation

Take the pad and draw on it a large sixteen-square grid with your black marking pen and a ruler. At the top of the pad where you have folded over the cover of the pad, write the following four sets of numbers lightly with the blue pencil: (7, 10, 13+) (12+, 1, 6, 11) (2, 15+, 8, 5) (9, 4, 3, 14+). They should be written small so that they can only be seen up close by you and not by anyone sitting in the audience. These figures are there to prompt you in case you forget any of them when you're writing down the magic square.

Presentation

The key to creating this type of Magic Square is knowing a secret mathematical formula. Fig. 88 illustrates how the magic square for the number 47 was generated. (Remember that you can create a magic square with any number greater than 40. However, it's suggested that you use a two-figure number.) Start with the number 47. Subtract 30 from it, and then divide the difference (17) by 4. This will leave you with a dividend of 4 and a remainder of 1.

Next, look at Fig. 89. In each one of the squares (except square D) you will find a number in a circle. This is the initial value of the square. You must add the dividend (4) to this value to get the final value for the square. For square D, enter only the value of the dividend (4). In the four squares that

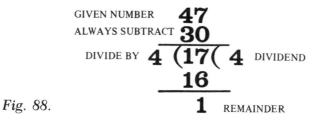

GIVEN NUMBER **47**
ALWAYS SUBTRACT **30**
DIVIDE BY **4 (17(4** DIVIDEND
16

Fig. 88. **1** REMAINDER

A	B	C	D
⑦	⑩	⑬+	
E	**F**	**G**	**H**
⑫+	①	⑥	⑪
I	**J**	**K**	**L**
②	⑮+	⑧	⑤
M	**N**	**O**	**P**
⑨	④	③	⑭+

Fig. 89.

have a plus sign (+) next to the circled initial amount (squares
C, E, J, P), also add the remainder (1) from your calculation to
get the final value for the square.

Our sample square would thus be created as follows: (A) 7
+ 4 = 11; (B) 10 + 4 = 14; (C) 13 + 4 + 1 = 18; (D) 0 + 4
= 4; (E) 12 + 4 + 1 = 17; (F) 1 + 4 = 5; (G) 6 + 4 = 10;
(H) 11 + 4 = 15; (I) 2 + 4 = 6; (J) 15 + 4 + 1 = 20; (K) 8 +
4 = 12; (L) 5 + 4 = 9; (M) 9 + 4 = 13; (N) 4 + 4 = 8;
(O) 3 + 4 = 7; (P) 14 + 4 + 1 = 19.

You can make up squares for very large numbers, for example, the year you were born. With a little practice, and some
memorizing, you'll be able to do this mental feat very quickly.

In the **Preparation** section, you were instructed to pencil
four sets of numbers at the top of the pad on the inside of the
front cover. Each set of numbers is a reminder of the numeric

values assigned to the four rows of squares: A, B, C, D; E, F, G, H; I, J, K, L; and M, N, O, P.

Fig. 90 shows the completed magic square in our example. Good luck on mastering this feat of mental agility!

THIS MAGIC SQUARE HAS BEEN ELECTRONICALLY COMPUTED BY THE MAC COMPUTER TO TOTAL 47 WHEN ADDED IN ANY DIRECTION. THE COMBINATIONS ARE:

A, B, C, D	E, F, G, H
I, J, K, L	M, N, O, P
A, F, K, P	M, J, G, D
A, D, M, P	F, G, J, K
I, J, M, N	A, B, E, F
C, D, G, H	K, L, O, P
E, I, H, L	B, C, N, O
A, E, I, M	B, F, J, N
C, G, K, O	D, H, L, P

A 11	B 14	C 18	D 4
E 17	F 5	G 10	H 15
I 6	J 20	K 12	L 9
M 13	N 8	O 7	P 19

Fig. 90.

A THOUGHT-TRANSFERENCE TRICK

· ·

Effect

Tell the audience that you and your assistant will perform an experiment concerning Second Sight. Tell your assistant to sit on a chair in a corner of the room facing the wall, and then ask someone from the audience to blindfold your assistant. Now have the person who blindfolded your assistant walk around the room and touch an object. Let's say he touches a vase. Ask your blindfolded assistant, "Did he touch the lamp? The piano? The chair? The rug? The vase?" At this point, the assistant replies, "Yes, it was the vase that was touched!"

You and your assistant should continue in this manner,

identifying five or six more objects touched by members of the audience. Never change the tone of your voice or make any other noise that could possibly convey a message to your blindfolded assistant. Is this truly a case of Second Sight?

Presentation

No, it's not Second Sight, but only the use of a clever prearranged code. Before the performance, get together with your assistant and work out the following verbal code: Agree that the object touched will be the second one you mention after you name an object that starts with the letter C. In the example just given, the first C object that you, the magician, asked about was a chair. Two objects later, you mentioned the vase.

You and your assistant should agree on a set of key letters to be used. This way, when you repeat the trick, begin the key word with a different letter each time, to throw off the audience. A little practice beforehand will ensure a successful performance and should leave your audience wondering how in the world you did it.

LIGHTNING ADDITION
· ·

Effect

In this mental masterpiece, you will show your audience that you can add up a column of numbers before it's even written down. Get someone from the audience to help you with this one. On a large blackboard, or drawing pad, write down the number 234. Have your assistant write any three-digit number under it. Now write a three-digit number under his. Continue doing this three more times, at which point he has written down four numbers and you have written five. Now draw a line under the column and have him add the numbers up. He'll come up with the number 4,230. Point to an envelope on your table and tell him to open it. Inside he'll find a sheet of paper with "The total of the numbers will be 4,230" written on it.

Materials Needed

An envelope with the total written down on a piece of paper inside

A large blackboard or drawing pad

Presentation

Obviously, you are going to control the column of numbers so that the final total will be 4,230. The first number that you wrote down was your key number. The next eight numbers were written down in a series of four pairs; first the assistant would write a number and then you would write another number under it. Every number you write under the one he has written will, when added to his, give you a total of 999. Here's an example of how it would look:

$$
\begin{array}{rl}
(1) & 234 \\
(2) & 321 \\
(3) & 678 \\
(4) & 972 \\
(5) & 027 \\
(6) & 321 \\
(7) & 678 \\
(8) & 422 \\
(9) & 577 \\
\hline
\text{Total} & 4{,}230
\end{array}
$$

You'll notice that the pairs of numbers 2-3, 4-5, 6-7, and 8-9 each total 999. In other words, when he wrote down 321 you wrote 678 under it. Added together, they total 999.

If you were to take the key number that you wrote first, 234, and subtract 4 from it, you would get the last three numbers of the total. Also, if you then took that 4 and placed it in front of the number, you would then have 4,230, the total. The reason that we subtract 4 from the key number is that 4 represents the number of paired numbers we wrote under the key number.

Knowing how the key number works allows you to repeat the trick using a different key number, thus giving you a different total every time.

Paper Magic

THE BEELZEBUB PAPER TRICK

Effect

Your friends will think that this is a Devil of a trick if you do it well. Pass a length of rope and a stiff piece of paper in the shape of a bell to your audience for examination. Next, have someone thread the bell onto the rope and then have him tie each end of the rope to your wrists (Fig. 91). You can even have him seal the knots with tape. Last, have him drape a large cloth over your arms so that your hands, the rope, and the bell are out of sight. In ten seconds flat, drop the cloth and show that the paper bell has been removed undamaged from the rope and that your hands are still securely tied. The rope and bell may once more be examined.

Materials Needed

One piece of rope three feet long
Two identical paper bells
A large cloth about three feet square

Preparation

Place one of the paper bells in your shirt pocket under your jacket.

Presentation

Everything occurs as described above up to the point where the cloth is placed over your arms. At this point, raise your arms chest high. Under cover of the cloth, tear the bell off the rope, crumple it up, and slip it into your inside jacket pocket. Remove the other paper bell from your shirt pocket and drop it on the table. Shake the cloth off your arms, and the trick is done. Another version of the trick would be to try secreting the second bell up the sleeve of your jacket instead of in your shirt pocket. This way, you wouldn't have to raise your arms up to your chest.

Fig. 91.

A PAPER MAGNET

....

Effect

"Yes, Ladies and Gentlemen, you heard me correctly: a paper magnet is both a possibility and a fact! Watch closely while I demonstrate this new wonder of science. First, I take this pencil and draw a picture of a magnet on this small piece of cardboard [Fig. 92]. Next, I cut a 2-inch piece from this paper straw and place it on the table. To magnetize the paper magnet, I rub it vigorously back and forth on a piece of cloth to build up a charge of static electricity.

"I now place the magnet on the table just in front of the paper straw. Watch this: As I move the magnet away from the straw, the straw follows it. Did you see that? Here, I'll do it once more before the magnet loses its power. There goes the straw again. It's amazing what new discoveries are made in science every day."

Fig. 92.

Materials Needed

A pencil
One small piece of cardboard

A paper straw
A piece of cloth

Presentation

The cardboard magnet isn't really magnetized. When the performer bends over the table and draws the card away from the straw, he opens his lips slightly and gently blows a stream of air down onto the table just behind the straw (Fig. 93). A little practice will show you just how easy it is to make the piece of straw appear to be following the card across the table. You can also present this as a puzzle and see how long it takes your audience to discover how you make the straw move.

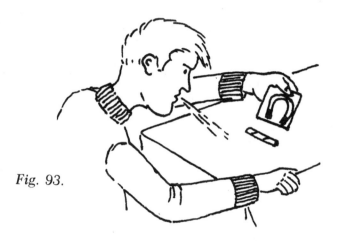

Fig. 93.

Try not to purse your lips when you blow down on the table, as this can give the secret away. Just part your lips slightly when you blow on the straw. A steady flow of chatter and a lot of hand movement will help to distract your audience from seeing how you're really making the straw move.

THE HEAVEN-AND-HELL
PAPER TRICK

This is a great bit of magic that can be done with a single sheet of paper. Present the following story to your audience:

"I once heard a story concerning greed that I would like to pass on to you. It seems that two souls confronted St. Peter at the gates of Heaven and asked to come in. St. Peter told them that there was but room for one of them and that they must therefore draw lots to see who was the worthiest. St. Peter then took a sheet of paper and folded it once, and then once again, and finally a third time. [Figs. 94–97]. He then tore the folded sheet of paper into two unequal portions [Fig. 98] and

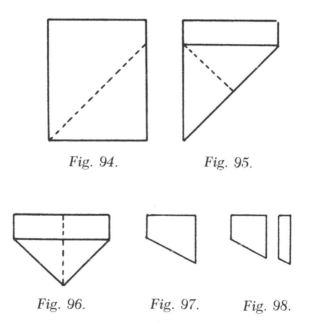

Fig. 94.   Fig. 95.

Fig. 96.   Fig. 97.   Fig. 98.

was about to speak when one of the two souls knocked the other aside and reached out and grabbed the larger portion of paper. 'I have the bigger piece,' he shouted. 'I won, let me in!'

"'Quiet,' commanded St. Peter, 'let us see what these lots

have to tell us. The smaller piece belongs to this gentleman who has yet to speak. If we open it up, we find that it is in the shape of a cross [Fig. 99]. Now, let me have the piece that you so rudely took from me. Before we open it up, we will tear it down the middle [Fig. 100]. Now, we'll open up the pieces and see what they have to tell you.'

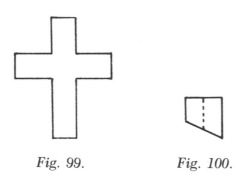

Fig. 99.   Fig. 100.

"When the pieces were opened up, the hasty man found that they formed the word *HELL* [Fig. 101]. Seeing his fate clearly written before him the man turned to go, but St. Peter bade him enter along with the other man, saying, 'There is always room for one more up here, and I can see from this lesson that greed has been driven out of your heart for good.' I'd say that's a pretty good lesson for all of us."

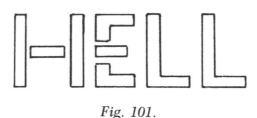

Fig. 101.

THE FANTASTIC FIR TREE

Effect

Take five or six sheets of newspaper and roll them into a tight tube while telling your audience a few jokes to keep their attention. At the conclusion of the jokes, turn this tube into a six-foot-high fir tree.

Materials Needed

Five or six strips of newspaper twelve inches in width, cut
 from several double-sheets of newspaper
A rubber band

Presentation

Take one of the strips and start rolling it up into a cylinder. When you get to the last 5 inches of the strip, overlap another sheet (Fig. 102) and keep on rolling. Do this with each of the remaining sheets until the tube is complete.

Snap a rubber band around the tube near the bottom. Flatten out the tube and tear it down the center. Stop about two-thirds of the way down (Fig. 103).

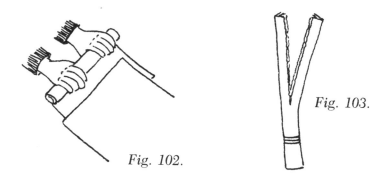

Fig. 102.

Fig. 103.

Flatten out the tube on the other side and tear it again the same way (Fig. 104). Bend the four sections of strips down along the sides of the tube (Fig. 105). Take hold of the tube with one hand, and with the other reach into the center of the tube and take hold of a few of the strips. Gently pull them up and out of the tube. Keep pulling and working the strips upward (Fig. 106). You will end up with a paper fir tree about five or six feet high, depending on how many strips of paper you used to make the tube.

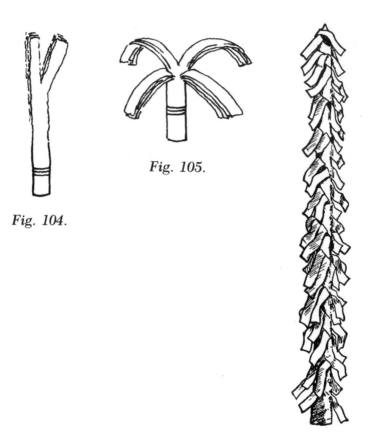

Fig. 105.

Fig. 104.

Fig. 106.

Rope Magic

THE HINDU BANGLE TRICK

Fig. 107.

Effect

From the fabled regions of the Indian subcontinent comes the Hindu Bangle Trick, which, when performed well, is truly amazing. Follow closely the details of its presentation.

Ask someone to come forward from the audience to assist you. Hand him a stout length of rope, about two and a half feet in length, and have him tie both ends of the rope to your wrists (Fig. 108). The knots should be very tight and even sealed with tape to heighten the effect.

Next, hand your assistant a plastic ring some four inches in diameter. Instruct him to pass it among the audience to verify that it is not a trick ring or has been tampered with in any

Fig. 108.

way. When he returns the ring to you, instruct him to drape a three-foot-square cloth over your hands and arms. Then tell him to step back and slowly count to five. At the count of five, let the cloth slip to the floor; the audience will see that the ring is now threaded on the rope. On examination, your wrists are found to be securely bound (Fig. 109). Instruct your assistant to cut you free, and step back to acknowledge the thunderous applause.

Fig. 109.

Materials Needed

Two matching bangles
A three-foot-square cloth
A stout, two-and-a-half-foot length of rope

Presentation

How is this trick accomplished? When you go to the magic store (Woolworth's of course), buy two matching bangles. When you present this trick, the second one is already on your arm, halfway up your sleeve. Under cover of the cloth, slip your hand up your sleeve and bring the bangle down. Hold this bangle with one hand while slipping the first bangle (the one you showed to the audience) with your other hand onto a hook inside your coat. Or, slip the ring back up the sleeve of your coat and get rid of it as soon as possible.

HERE, THERE, EVERYWHERE

Effect

All that is needed to perform this rope trick is a four-foot length of rope and an eight-inch-diameter wooden embroidery ring. (Any large, solid ring will do.) Pick up a piece of rope and show it to the audience. There are three knots tied in the rope. The solid wooden ring hangs on one of the end knots (Fig. 110). Pass the rope behind your back, and the ring will jump to the knot at the other end of the rope (Fig. 111). Once again pass the rope behind your back, and the ring jumps back to the other end (Fig. 110). The third time you do this, however, the ring is found to have jumped to the middle knot (Fig. 112). Immediately hand the rope, with the ring still securely tied to the middle knot, out for inspection.

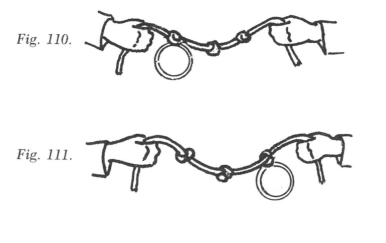

Fig. 110.

Fig. 111.

Fig. 112.

The secret lies in the fact that there is a fourth knot tied in the rope. This knot is hidden by your hand, which covers the knot when you hold the rope (Fig. 113). Also, the bottom knot on the rope is a slip knot (Fig. 114).

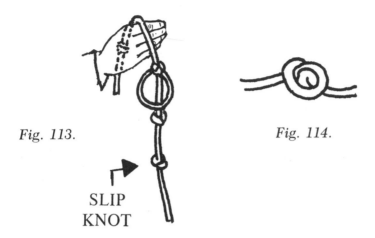

Fig. 113.   Fig. 114.

SLIP
KNOT

Presentation

Pick up the rope with your right hand, remembering to conceal the extra knot (Fig. 113), and hold it up to the audience (Fig. 110). When you pass the rope behind your back, cover the end with the extra knot with your left hand. Then show the rope to the audience (Fig. 111). The previous action is reversed for the next pass. During the final pass behind your back, pull the rope tight so that slip knot will come apart and disappear. Now bring the rope out. The ring will be on the middle knot. A perfect deception.

THE MIRACLE ROPE TRICK

Here is a method for restoring a cut rope that will leave your friends truly baffled. To perform it, you will need an easily made gimmick. (A gimmick is an aid to performing a trick that your audience knows nothing about.) Cut a five-inch piece of rope from a clothesline. Make a loop of this piece and tape the ends together (Fig. 115).

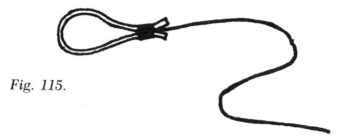

Fig. 115.

Next, attach a piece of elastic cord twelve inches or more in length, depending on how long your arm is, to the taped loop. Insert the loop and elastic into the right sleeve of your suit jacket and lower it until the end of the loop is about three inches from the end of the sleeve (Fig. 116). Take a safety pin

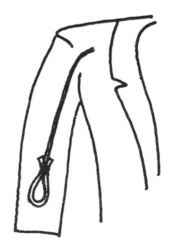

Fig. 116.

and attach the end of the elastic to the inside of your coat at the point where it enters the sleeve.

Now, put your coat on. Reach into the right sleeve with your left hand and pull the loop down into your right hand (Fig. 117). When performing this trick you must keep the back of your right hand to the audience at all times.

Fig. 117.

To perform, walk onto the stage with the loop already palmed in your right hand. With your right hand, pick up one end of a five-foot piece of clothesline from the table. With your left hand, pull the rope halfway through your right hand. Open your left hand and let the end of the rope drop. Reach into your right hand and apparently pull the middle of the rope up a couple of inches so that you can cut it into two pieces with a pair of scissors. What you are actually doing is pulling the concealed loop (the gimmick) up into view (Fig. 118).

Fig. 118.

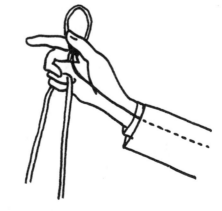

Now, cut this loop with the scissors. Replace the scissors on the table. With your left hand reach down, take the two ends of the rope, and place them in your right hand next to the two cut ends of the loop.

Now, say the appropriate magical incantation and throw the rope towards the ceiling. The moment you open up your hand to release the rope, the cut loop will fly up your sleeve, never to be seen again. It will appear that the rope has never been cut. The movement of your arm and the speed of the elastic will effectively screen the secret of the illusion from the eyes of your audience. Another amazing trick has been performed.

A KNOTTY PROBLEM

Effect

Stand before the audience and ask: "Did you ever have one of those days where everything seems to go wrong? Of course you have. The other day I was practicing tying some knots while I was working on a new escape trick. First, I tied a reef knot like this one, but when I pulled it tight it just disappeared. See, the same thing has happened with this knot.

"Next, I tried tying a Bulgarian Shoelace Knot, but when I went to pull it tight, it too disappeared just like this.

"Luckily, when I tried to tie a knot without letting go of either end my magic powers returned and I succeeded" (at this point, use the next trick in this chapter, the Impossible Knot).

Materials Needed

One three-foot length of soft rope

Presentation

Let's start with the first knot to disappear, the Reef Knot. Just follow the instructions in Figs. 119–121. When the knot is

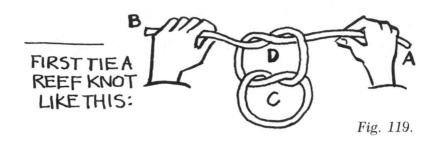

FIRST TIE A
REEF KNOT
LIKE THIS:

Fig. 119.

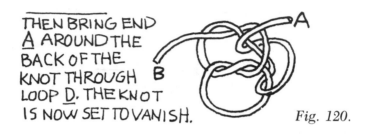

THEN BRING END
A AROUND THE
BACK OF THE
KNOT THROUGH
LOOP D. THE KNOT
IS NOW SET TO VANISH.

Fig. 120.

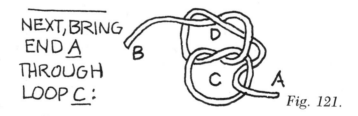

NEXT, BRING
END A
THROUGH
LOOP C:

Fig. 121.

made it looks formidable, but it will melt away like butter when you pull the ends apart.

The Bulgarian Shoelace Knot takes a bit more description. Place the rope over your hands as shown in Fig. 122. Clip the two loops between the first and second fingers of each hand and pull your hands apart (Fig. 123). Pull the rope tight and you will have formed a shoelace knot.

Next, reach through the right-hand loop with the thumb and first finger of your right hand and grasp end *B* of the rope (Fig. 124). Do the same with your left hand, grasping end *A*.

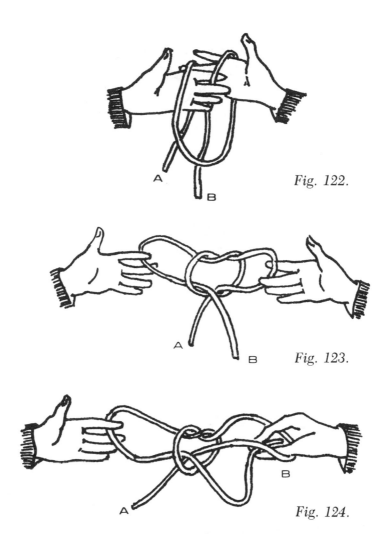

Fig. 122.

Fig. 123.

Fig. 124.

Pull the ends through the loops (Fig. 125) and pull the rope tight, forming a knot in the middle (Fig. 126). Pause a moment and then pull hard on the two ends. The knot will disappear in the twinkling of an eye (Fig. 127).

This presentation, in which you have failed to tie two different knots, is a perfect lead-in to the Impossible Knot trick.

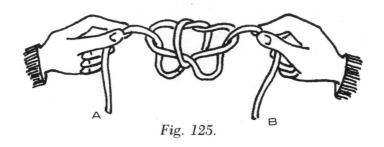

Fig. 125.

Fig. 126.

Fig. 127.

THE IMPOSSIBLE KNOT

Effect

Challenge someone in the audience to come forward and tie a
knot in a three-foot length of rope without letting go of either
end of the rope. After he has made a few unsuccessful at-
tempts, take the rope from him and proceed to show how it
can be done three different ways. This is a trick that violates
the axiom of never showing the same trick more than once to
the same audience.

Materials Needed

A three-foot length of soft rope
Transparent tape

Presentation

For the first method of tying, place the rope down on a table-top. Fold your arms in front of your chest and bend over the table. With your left hand, reach under your right arm and pick up the right end of the rope. With your right hand, reach over your left arm and pick up the left end of the rope.

Now, unfold your arms, drawing them apart. Stretch them far apart, and a knot will be formed in the center of the rope. This is method one.

For the second method, pick up the rope in both hands as shown in Fig. 128. Now, loop the rope over and behind your left wrist as shown in Fig. 129. Continue looping by weaving the end around the back strand as shown in Figs. 129 and 130. When you're finished, your hands, palms up, should look like the hands shown in Fig. 131.

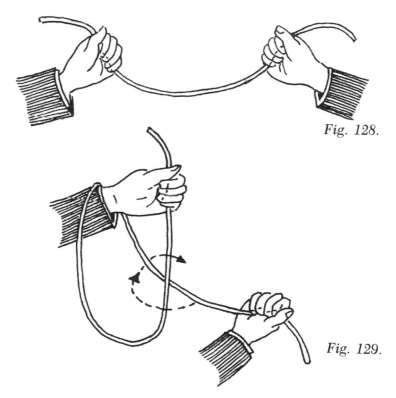

Fig. 128.

Fig. 129.

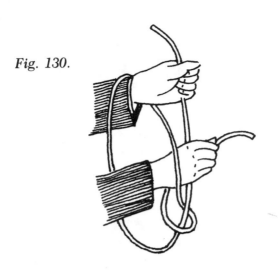

Fig. 130.

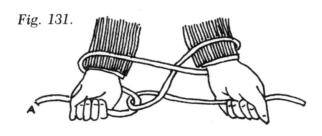

Fig. 131.

Now comes the important move of the trick. Turn both palms down, letting the loops slide off the back of your hands. However, when you do this your right hand should let go of rope end A and grasp the rope at point C. As the loops slide off your hands, rope end A slides through loop B; this allows you to stretch your arms apart, thus forming a knot in the center of the rope (Fig. 132). The action is so fast that the audience cannot see you releasing and then regrasping the end of the rope.

At this point, pause and pretend to see a look of doubt in one or two faces in the audience. Then say, "I think that one or two of you are still not convinced that I can indeed tie a knot in a rope without letting go of either end. Very well, I will

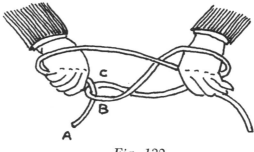

Fig. 132.

show you once again, but this time I will do it under test conditions!"

Now have the gentleman who first assisted you take the transparent tape and firmly tape each end of the rope to your first fingers (Fig. 133). When this is done, repeat the previous steps up through and including Fig. 131. At this point say, "I have just completed the knot, but you cannot see it. To prove it, I want this gentleman to remove the ends of the rope from my fingers and to then stretch the rope apart. There, you see! There is a knot in the middle just as I said there would be. I've shown you how to do this feat three different ways. Now go home and entertain your friends with this amazing bit of rope magic!"

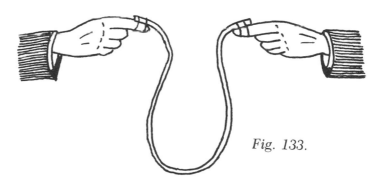

Fig. 133.

THE IMPOSSIBLE LINKING ROPES

· ·

Effect

You, the magician, will perform the seemingly impossible task of linking together two pieces of rope while they are hidden under a handkerchief.

Materials Needed

Two three-foot lengths of rope. One rope is white, and the other is dyed red.

One heavy pocket handkerchief

Presentation

Place the two lengths of rope on the table in front of you. Loop each rope in the form of a U and place them side-by-side as shown in Fig. 134. The loop ends should be towards you.

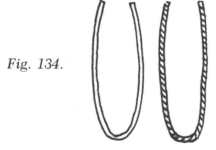

Fig. 134.

Next, open up a heavy white pocket handkerchief and drape it over the two ropes, leaving the ends exposed (Fig. 135). Now, reach under the handkerchief and tell your audience that you are causing the ropes to link together. What you are doing is to pull one side of the red rope over the nearer side of the white rope, and then to tuck the red rope back under, as shown in Fig. 135.

A moment later, bring your hands out and take hold of the bottom ends of the handkerchief. Then draw the handkerchief

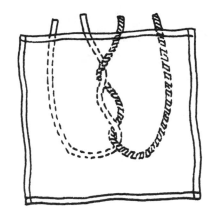

Fig. 135.

away from you until the linked loops of the rope come into view (Fig. 136). Keep moving the cloth down until the ends of the rope are covered.

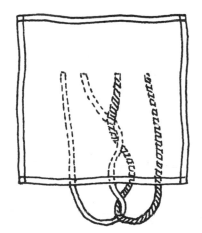

Fig. 136.

Move your hands back to the top of the cloth, and then pick up the two linked ropes and the handkerchief as one and hold it up in front of you (Fig. 137). At this point the cords will untangle themselves automatically behind the cloth. After three or four seconds, let the handkerchief drop to the table. Lay the two linked ropes down on the table in front of you and elaborate on the impossibility that the audience has just witnessed.

Fig. 137.

THE IMPOSSIBLE ROPE TRICK

Effect

To the audience, this will seem to be truly an "impossible" rope trick. Display to the audience three pieces of rope, all of different lengths. Then cause the shortest piece to grow in length and the longest piece to shrink until all the pieces are of the same length. After showing each piece to the audience, cause the pieces of rope to return to their original lengths. Then immediately pass out the three pieces for examination.

Materials Needed

Three pieces of rope. The short piece should be 12″ long, the medium piece 28″, and the long piece 42″.

Presentation

Hold up the short piece of rope and place it in your left hand. Next, exhibit the long piece and place this in your left hand. Last, show the medium piece and place this too in your left hand (Fig. 138). Keep the back of your left hand turned towards the audience.

Bring the end of the medium-length rope up so that it is next to its other end. Then bring the end of the short piece up and cross it over the end of the long piece that is held in your left hand. Finally, bring the end of the long piece up and over the loop of the short piece (Fig. 139).

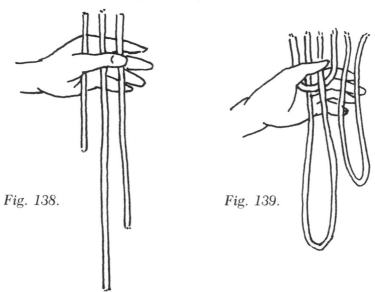

Fig. 138.

Fig. 139.

Now you are ready to cause all of the ropes to assume the same length. Reach over with your right hand and take hold of one end of the medium-length rope, the end to the right. Also, take hold of the two ends of the long rope. Your left hand is now holding the left end of the medium-length rope and both ends of the short-length rope. At this point, the short rope and the long rope are looped together. This is hidden from the audience by the back of the left hand.

Grip the ropes tightly with both hands and start to move your hands apart (Fig. 140). Keep moving your hands apart until the ropes appear to be the same length (Fig. 141). Let go of the ends in your right hand. You are now holding the three ropes in your left hand, and they all appear to be of the same length.

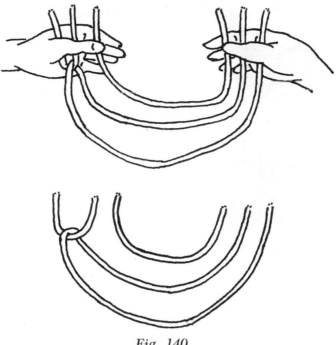

Fig. 140.

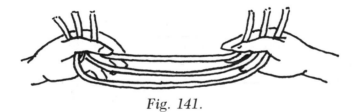

Fig. 141.

At this point, count the ropes, apparently showing each one of them individually. First, reach over and take hold of the medium length of rope and pull it away from your left hand (Fig. 142). Count, "One!"

Then bring your right hand back to get the second rope. What you are actually doing is taking the two ends of the short rope in your right thumb and forefinger and clipping the medium-length rope with the forefinger and index finger of

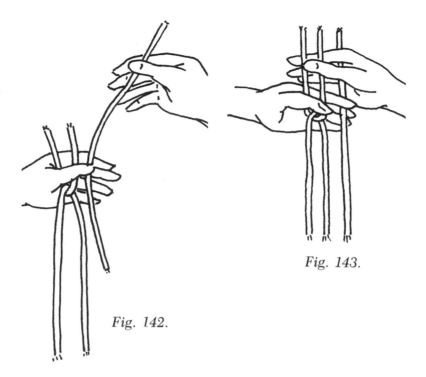

Fig. 142.

Fig. 143.

your left hand (Fig. 143). When you move your hands apart, you are holding the looped short and long pieces in your right hand and the medium piece in your left hand (Fig. 144). To the audience it will appear that you placed a second piece of rope into your right hand. Count aloud, "Two!" Through all of this,

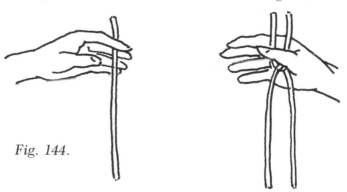

Fig. 144.

the loop between the two ropes is concealed by both your left and right hands. Both are at all times turned towards the audience.

Finally, move your right hand back and use it to draw the medium-length rope through the fingers of your left hand (Fig. 145). Count aloud, "Three!"

At this point, you have caused the three ropes to become equal in length. To finish the trick, you now have to make them return to their original lengths. Transfer the ropes from your right hand to your left hand (Fig. 146). Make sure that the loop is not seen.

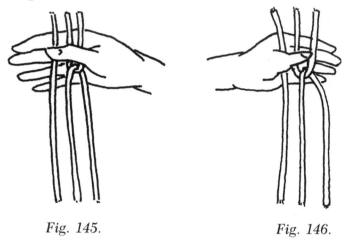

Fig. 145.   Fig. 146.

Take the dangling ends of the ropes, one by one, and position them in your left hand, as shown in Fig. 147. The ends of each rope should end up being side-by-side in your hand. Now, slowly take hold of one of the ends of the short rope and pull on it until the short rope comes free from your left hand. Make sure that the loop is not drawn up into view. Toss the rope to the audience. Next, draw the medium-length rope from your hand and toss it to the audience. Finally, display the long rope and pass it out for examination.

Thus ends the perfect rope trick. There are no "extra" pieces to dispose of; the ropes are genuine, and everything can be examined once the trick is concluded.

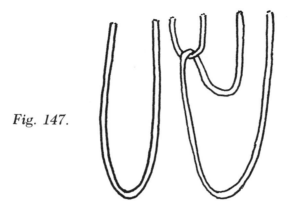

Fig. 147.

A ONE-HANDED KNOT TIE

Effect

Have someone from the audience assist you with this one. Hand him a three-foot length of rope and ask him to tie a knot in it with one hand. His attempt to do this will provoke a few laughs. Take another piece of rope and tell him that you will show him two simple ways in which to do this. First, lay the rope on the table, making a circle in the middle. Reach under the loop thus formed and take hold of one end of the rope and pull it through the loop, forming a knot in the rope. That's easy enough. The second method takes a little practice.

Materials

Two three-foot lengths of rope

Presentation

The secret for the second method involves four easy steps. In step one, drape the rope across your right hand, between your thumb and forefinger and behind your little finger (Fig. 148). The end of the rope, marked A in Fig. 148, should be longer than end B. In step two, give a little upward jerk to the rope and quickly drop your hand down towards end A. Catch the

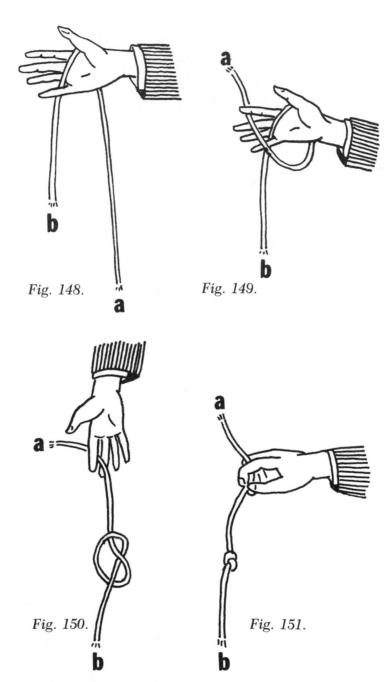

Fig. 148.

Fig. 149.

Fig. 150.

Fig. 151.

end of the rope (A) between the first two fingers of your hand (Fig. 149).

In step three, clip end A tightly between your fingers and turn your hand down so that the rest of the rope slips off your hand, forming a knot (Fig. 150). In the final step (Fig. 151), give the rope a quick jerk so that the knot is tightened in the center of the rope.

All four steps should be done quickly and smoothly. A little practice and you'll have a very pretty rope flourish to add to your act.

A MYSTERIOUS ROPE ESCAPE

Effect

Request that two members of the audience assist you in this effect. Ask one of them to remove his jacket. Then thread 2 eight-foot lengths of rope through the arms of the jacket, and instruct the assistant to put the jacket back on and button it. The ends of each rope should hang out of the sleeves. Take one end of rope from each sleeve and tie a single overhand knot with the ends in front of the assistant. Hand two ends of the ropes to the second assistant while retaining the other two ends in your hands. On the count of three, you and the assistant should both pull on the ropes sharply. To the amazement of all, the ropes will pass completely through the body and the coat of the first assistant.

Materials Needed

Two eight-foot lengths of soft nylon rope
A short piece of white thread

Preparation

Lay the eight-foot lengths of rope out on the table and tie them together in the middle with the piece of white thread (Fig. 152). Loop the thread around the ropes two or three times for strength.

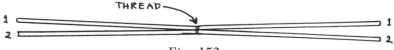

Fig. 152.

Presentation

Pick up the two pieces of rope in your right hand and show them to your audience. The middle of the ropes should be in the palm of your hand (Fig. 153). Tell the audience that you are about to show them a very old rope escape that baffled Houdini. Ask two gentlemen from the audience to come forward to assist you. Make sure that one of them is wearing a jacket. Have them stand to your left, and ask the gentleman with the jacket to remove it.

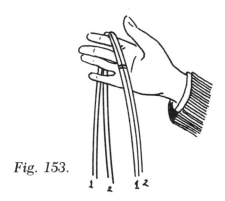

Fig. 153.

While the gentleman is taking his jacket off, transfer the ropes from your right hand to your left hand. During this transfer, insert your left thumb between the ropes on one side of the white thread that holds the ropes together, and the last three fingers of your left hand between the ropes on the other side of the white thread. When you take away the rope in your left hand, the ropes will now be "linked" together by the white thread (Figs. 154 and 155). In Fig. 155, the fingers are open to show you how this looks. During the performance keep your hand closed, with the back of it towards your audi-

Fig. 154.

Fig. 155.

ence. Practice this move so that it appears natural and you can do it without looking at your hands.

Take the jacket from the assistant and hold it up by the collar with your left hand. At all times the link that holds the ropes together must be covered by your hands. With your right hand, open up the side of the coat and ask the assistant to take the two ends of the rope (ends 1 and 1) and push them through the sleeve of the jacket until they come out the bottom (Fig. 156). Then reach over with your right hand and take the collar of the coat from your left hand, along with the ropes. Make sure that your hands cover the point where the ropes are linked together.

Next, open up the other side of the jacket with your left hand and tell the assistant to take the other two ends of the ropes (ends 2 and 2) and push them through the left sleeve until they too come out the bottom. When this is done, step behind the assistant and help him put his jacket back on. Hold the ropes, at the collar, tightly in your hand until his arms are

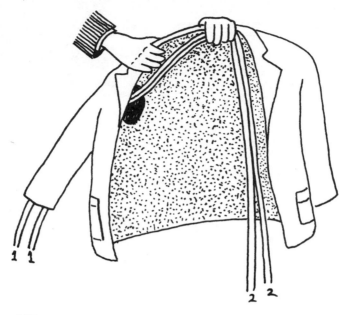

Fig. 156.

completely through the sleeves of the coat. This will prevent him from taking hold of the ropes in the sleeves and pulling them down, thus prematurely breaking the thread that holds them together.

Once your assistant's jacket is back on, have him button it up. Now, reach over and take one rope from each sleeve and tie them together with a single overhand knot in front of his jacket (Fig. 157). Have the second assistant stand on one side of him, while you stand on the other. Hand the second assistant two ends of the ropes (ends 1 and 2); you take the other two ends in your hands. On the count of three, you both should pull sharply on the cords. The thread will break, releasing the two ropes behind the first assistant's back. The cords will slide down and out of the sleeves, and the escape will be complete.

Fig. 157.

The props for this mystery are simple; they can be examined after the trick is over, and not a clue is left to reveal the secret. This trick is amazing enough to perform in your parlor or on the stage.

Coin Magic

THE DISSOLVING COIN

. . . .

Effect

Drop a coin into a half-full glass of water that is hidden by a handkerchief. Remove the handkerchief and the coin will be seen lying at the bottom of the glass. Cover the glass once again and ask a member of the audience to remove it from your hand and place it on the table. Then announce that the coin has now been dissolved by the water. When your assistant removes the handkerchief, he will find that the coin has indeed disappeared.

Materials Needed

A small, straight-sided six-ounce water glass, half filled
    with water
A quarter
A white handkerchief

Presentation

Place a handkerchief across the upturned palm of your right hand. Next, place the quarter in the center of the cloth, gripping it through the fabric with the thumb and forefinger of your right hand. Then turn your right hand over, letting the cloth drape down.

With your left hand, pick up the half-filled glass of water and hold it under the cloth. As soon as the cloth covers the glass, tilt the glass towards yourself. When the glass is in position, drop the coin in the handkerchief so that it hits the outside of the glass and comes to rest in your outstretched fingertips (Fig. 158). The sound of the coin striking the glass will convince the audience that the coin has fallen into the

Fig. 158.

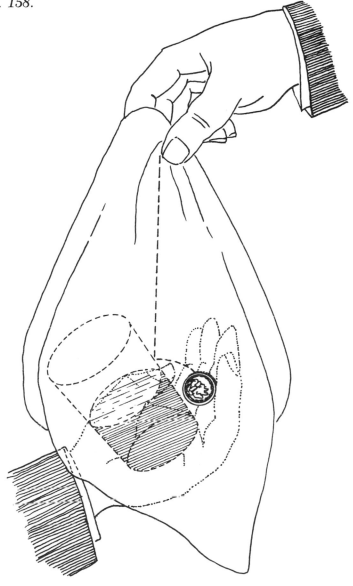

glass. Let the handkerchief settle over the rim of the glass while adjusting the glass in your left hand so that it now covers the quarter in the palm of your hand.

Now, remove the handkerchief and allow the audience to look down into the water, where the quarter will be visible at the bottom of the glass. It will look as though the coin is indeed under the water.

Once again, cover the glass and instruct someone to take the glass off your hand and place it on the table, still covered. The moment that the glass is gripped by your assistant, let go of the glass, close your hand, and remove it from under the handkerchief, palming the coin as you move it to the edge of the table in front of you. As you make the comment about the coin having been melted by the water, let the coin drop into your lap and then move your left hand back to point to the glass.

When the cloth has been removed, the coin will be gone and your hands will be empty. Practice this a great deal before performing. Once you've mastered the moves, you'll have an outstanding mystery to fool your friends with.

INDEX

About the Author

In the area of puzzles, games, and magic, Charles Barry Townsend is one of our more prolific authors. To date, he has written 14 books on these subjects, including *The World's Best Magic Tricks*, *The World's Best Puzzles*, *The World's Most Challenging Puzzles*, *The World's Toughest Puzzles*, *The World's Most Baffling Puzzles*, and *The World's Hardest Puzzles*. He currently lives with his family in Hilton Head, South Carolina.

Charles Barry Townsend and his dog, Jackie, working on a new trick called "The Floating Dog Bone Illusion."